Creative
WALLPAPER

Creative
WALLPAPER

Ideas & Projects
for Walls, Furniture
& Home Accessories

Lyna Farkas
Paige Gilchrist

LARK BOOKS
A Division of Sterling Publishing Co., Inc.
New York

Editor: Paige Gilchrist
Art Director: Tom Metcalf
Photographer: Wright Creative Photography & Design
Cover Designer: Barbara Zaretsky
Illustrator: Bernadette Wolf
Assistant Editor: Veronika Gunter
Production Assistance: Avery Johnson
Editorial Assistance: Delores Gosnell
Editorial Interns: Jason McGill and Brian Smith

Special Photography
Sanoma Syndication: Alexander van Borge, Dennis Brandsma, John Dummer, Hotze Eisme, Luuk Geertsen, Jon van Groenedaal, Paul Grootes, Louis Lemaire, Patrick van de Sande, Hans Zeegers.

Cover: Photo lower left, Sanoma Syndication; lower right, Today Interiors, courtesy of Gaetano, gaetano-usa.com
Back cover: Photo far left, lower, courtesy of Waverly Wallcoverings, a division of F. Schumacher & Co.; top left and lower left, Today Interiors, courtesy of Gaetano, gaetano-usa.com; lower right, courtesy of Seabrook Wallcoverings, Inc.

The Library of Congress has cataloged the hardcover edition as follows:

Gilchrist, Paige.
  Creative wallpaper : ideas & projects for walls, furniture & home
accessories / by Paige Gilchrist & Lyna Farkas.
      p. cm.
Includes index.
 ISBN 1-57990-418-1
 1. Paperhanging. 2. Wallpaper. I. Farkas, Lyna. II. Title.
  TH8441.G54 2003
  698'.6--dc21

                              2003004698

10 9 8 7 6 5 4 3 2 1

Published by Lark Books, a division of
Sterling Publishing Co., Inc.
387 Park Avenue South, New York, N.Y. 10016

First Paperback Edition 2005
© 2003, Lark Books and Lyna Farkas

Distributed in Canada by Sterling Publishing, c/o Canadian Manda Group, 165 Dufferin Street, Toronto, Ontario, Canada M6K 3H6

Distributed in the U.K. by Guild of Master Craftsman Publications Ltd., Castle Place, 166 High Street, Lewes, East Sussex, England BN7 1XU
Tel: (+ 44) 1273 477374, Fax: (+ 44) 1273 478606, Email: pubs@thegmcgroup.com, Web: www.gmcpublications.com

Distributed in Australia by Capricorn Link (Australia) Pty Ltd., P.O. Box 704, Windsor, NSW 2756 Australia

If you have questions or comments about this book, please contact:
Lark Books
67 Broadway
Asheville, NC 28801
(828) 253-0467

Manufactured in China

ISBN 1-57990-418-1 (hardcover) 1-57990-743-1 (paperback)

For information about custom editions, special sales, premium and corporate purchases, please contact Sterling Special Sales Department at 800-805-5489 or specialsales@sterlingpub.com.

contents

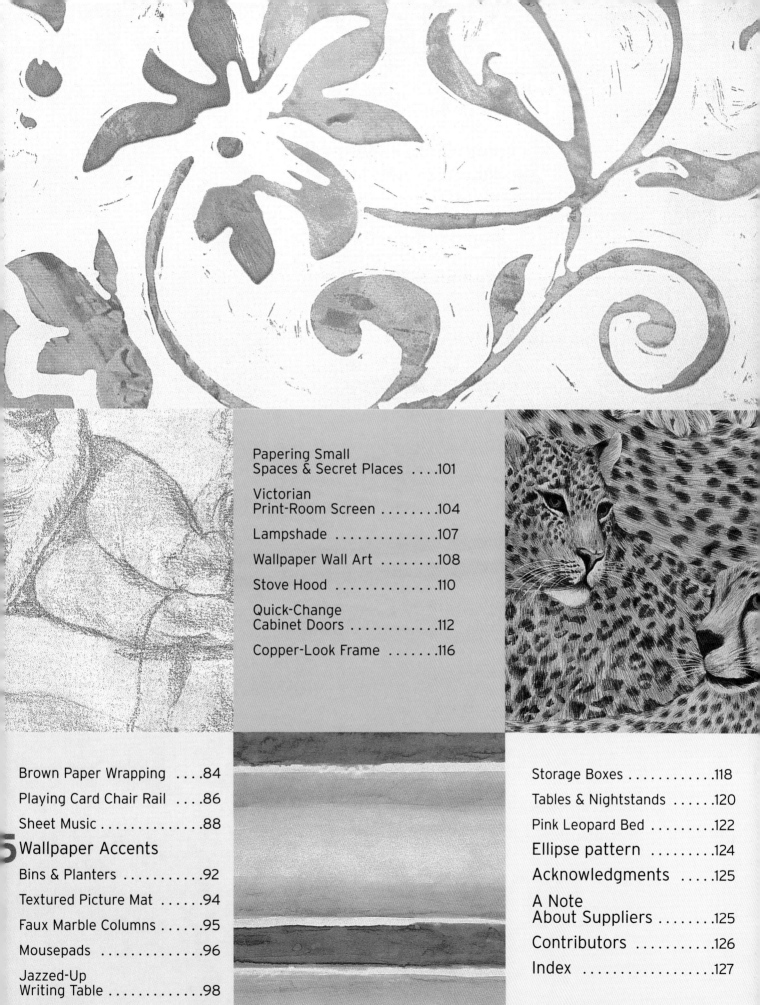

introduction

WELCOME TO THE NEW LOOK OF WALLPAPER AND ITS UPDATED ROLE IN CONTEMPORARY HOME DECOR.

SURE, YOU CAN STILL FIND ROLLS OF FUSSY, CUTESY, GAUDY, AND BUSY PAPERS OUT THERE. BUT TODAY, YOU'RE MUCH MORE LIKELY TO RUN ACROSS SAGE-COLORED STYLES THAT LOOK LIKE PARCHMENT, RICH DESIGNS FEATURING BRICK-RED WASHES, AND TEXTURED AND PAINTABLE PAPERS THAT IMITATE EVERYTHING FROM STUCCO TO HAND-HEWN WOOD. ORNATE AND FORMAL HAVE GIVEN WAY TO RELAXED, INDIVIDUAL, SIMPLE, AND DOWNRIGHT PLAYFUL. IN PLACE OF OVERPOWERING VICTORIAN PRINTS, YOU CAN FIND SUBTLE GILDED PAPERS. THE PUFFY BOUQUETS OF PEONIES THAT RAN UP AND DOWN YOUR GRANDMOTHER'S WALLS HAVE BEEN REPLACED WITH GRAPHIC, BLACK-AND-WHITE BLOOMS AND DELICATE BOTANICALS. AND, FOR A NEW LOOK ALL YOUR OWN, THERE'S EVERYTHING FROM SLEEK METALLIC STRIPES TO BOLD, COLORFUL POLKA DOTS.

THIS BOOK BEGINS BY TAKING YOU ON A FULL-COLOR TOUR OF HOW MUCH WALLPAPER HAS CHANGED. THEN, YOU'LL SEE HOW WALLPAPER'S RENEWED APPEAL ALSO HAS A WHOLE LOT TO DO WITH CHANGES IN HOW IT'S USED.

  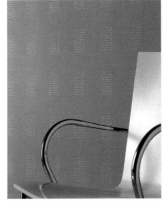

new ways to paper walls

Today's approaches are aimed at enhancing a setting rather than taking it over. Instead of covering every square inch of a room with a big, overwhelming pattern, you might use an understated print to tie the elements of a room together, a vibrant paper in just a few select spots to add a splash of personality, or a luxurious textured paper to infuse a room with warmth. You'll find projects for patchwork applications of coordinating papers, cut-and-paste wallpaper shapes, blending wallpaper with architectural elements, and more. There are also projects for interesting ceiling treatments, from making

your own wallpaper ceiling medallions to using embossed paper to create a faux tin-tile ceiling. And there's a feature on updated looks with wallpaper borders, plus steps for making your own.

alternative papers

Want to completely customize your walls? There's a full section of innovative ideas for covering them with something other than a commercially manufactured paper. If you wonder how materials as inexpensive and accessible as sheets of tissue paper or brown grocery bags can transform your walls into beautifully textured backgrounds, read on. You'll also find projects for personalizing your walls with everything from road maps and sheet music to Asian metallic-leaf paper and a deck of playing cards.

faces other than walls. You'll learn how to cover a stove hood, create your own mouse pads, use a distinctive paper to highlight a set of open display shelves, and add decorative touches to everything from a wooden headboard and a set of storage boxes to a picture frame and an elegant standing screen.

basic techniques

In Wallpapering Basics, you'll find step-by-step instructions, complete with how-to photos, for all the standard techniques for papering walls, from measuring your wallpaper strips and matching patterns to working around windows and doors. The instructions for each project tell you how to adapt these basics for more creative applications, alternative papers, and other surfaces.

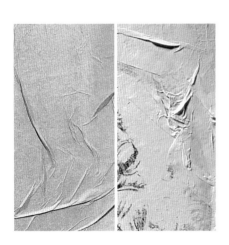

wallpaper accents

Soon after latching onto a few new wallpapers you adore, you may discover you're short on walls for them all—or you have leftover scraps you don't want to toss. That's where tables, lamps, cupboard doors, and nightstand drawers come in. This section is full of nearly two dozen projects that use small sections of paper to embellish all sorts of sur-

Whether you're reacquainting yourself with wallpaper or just discovering it, you're right on time for its comeback as a part of contemporary home decor. Here's a book full of projects and ideas that show you how to make the most of it—and give your walls and home accents a new look that's just right for the way you decorate today.

chapter 1

a tour of contemporary wallpapers

Get started with this vivid trip through wallpaper's fresh new looks. You'll see modern approaches to classics, such as florals, geometrics, and stripes. You'll also find brand new styles, from light-reflective papers to designs that imitate faux finishes. We give you samples of what's out there, and show you how they look in today's settings.

florals

Today's floral wallpapers feature everything from whispy botanicals and single petals to big, bold splashes of color.

pattern plays

The pattern you choose, even within a single wallpaper category such as florals, has a lot to do with the look you create.

• Small patterns are generally going to seem more sedate and create a subdued effect.

• Large ones will feel louder and more boisterous and often add drama.

• Tight patterns typically will look quieter and more sophisticated and emphasize color.

• Loose patterns will be more playful and emphasize the design of the pattern itself.

unify a setting

Wallpaper can help ease the transition from one room to another. If you have an open floor plan, where the living room and dining area adjoin, for example, or you have hallways or alcoves you want to connect to larger spaces, well-chosen wallpaper can be your link.

• Choose a wallpaper pattern for one room that coordinates closely with the upholstery in the next.

• Make the connection more subtle by working primarily with color. Use wallpaper with identical patterns in the two areas—maybe a full papering job in one and just an accent in the other—but vary the color of the paper in the two places. You can use different shades of the same color or choose two colors that coordinate.

• Use wallpaper to pull together or highlight specific design elements in a room, from upholstery patterns and colors to ornamental features on furniture.

• Choose wallpaper as you would any other decorative accent. If your room features ornate molding and arched windows, you might want a more formal-looking paper, maybe a silk or damask, with a neutral color and subtle pattern. To match lots of hardwood, a warm-colored textured paper might be better. In a room that shows off lots of modern geometric patterns, choose a wallpaper that's graphic and sleek, rather than one with swirls and fuss.

• Take furniture cushions, swatches of drapery fabric, carpet squares, and paint chips with you to the wallpaper store to better match your choices with the room's existing colors and patterns.

Far from the staid and heavy florals that gave wallpaper its bad rap, today's patterns feature huge photographic prints, panels of blossoms you can apply as wall art, and dramatic accents, such as a single strip of flowers running down a wall.

geometrics
& stripes

In their contemporary form, geometrics and stripes break out of rigid rows and subtle color schemes to show off looser, less formal styles, metallic finishes, bright colors, more sophisticated alternatives, and definite personality.

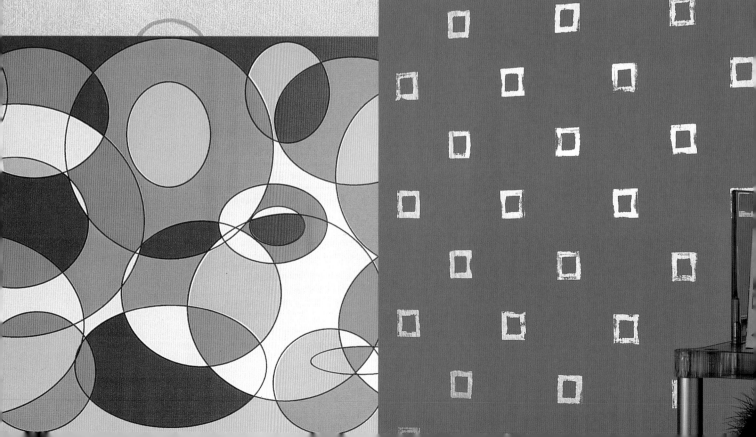

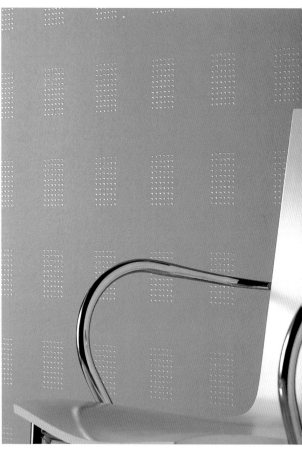

In this versatile category of wallpaper, you can find everything from broad, vertical stripes that set an elegant tone to crisp, horizontal bands perfect for clean, urban settings. You'll also see new interpretations of classic patterns such as polka dots and checks.

guiding the eye

One of the most useful reasons to choose a wallpaper with stripes is to help give a room the illusion of height or depth that it needs. A design with thin, vertical stripes running fairly closely together adds a sense of elevation to a setting. Wallpaper featuring sharp, horizontal stripes urges the eye to move with the lines, giving the setting a feeling of added depth.

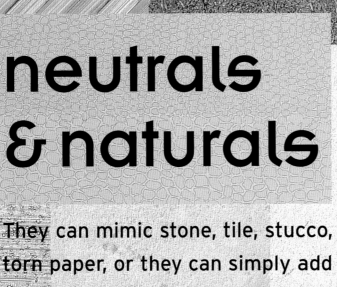

neutrals & naturals

They can mimic stone, tile, stucco, or torn paper, or they can simply add some understated but luxurious texture (and help mask imperfect walls). Either way, today's neutral and natural-look papers provide a subtle richness you just can't achieve with a plain coat of paint.

neutrals & naturals according to style

Consider your room's permanent features, such as its ceiling height and molding style, when you're choosing a neutral or natural paper to fit the scene. Also, play off the personality of the accents you already have in place, whether sheer drapes or concrete countertops.

Peaceful

If your room includes features such as blond wood, billowy curtains, whitewash, or lots of natural light, pick papers that resemble marble, color washes, or light-colored stone, or try natural-colored grass cloths.

Urban

Pair stainless steel, metal shelving, and glass blocks with papers that create the look of concrete, stucco, or texturized stone.

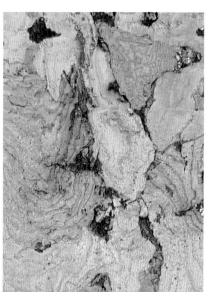
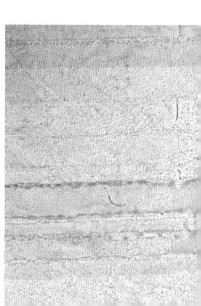

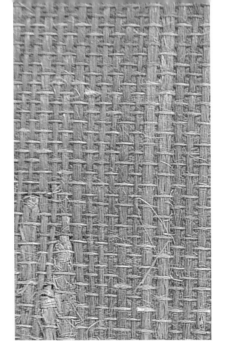
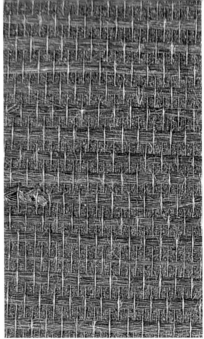
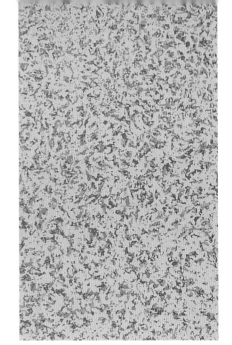

Rustic
For a room with exposed beams, woven rugs, hardwood floors, or a stone fireplace, consider wallpapers that offer the look of brick or wood.

Exotic
If your decor has hints of an Asian tearoom, Spanish villa, or something similar, try papers that replicate tile, stucco, or bamboo, or experiment with some of the more elaborate and rich-colored grass cloths.

faux-finish effects

Painted faux finishes, from stamping, stenciling, and sponging to marbling and combing, have become wildly popular in interior design, thanks to the variety, color, and dimension they add to any surface. Now, even if you haven't mastered the painting techniques, you can achieve the look with wallpapers that come in every faux-finish style imaginable.

color play

In addition to giving careful thought to pattern and style, keep in mind that the color of your wallpaper can have a huge impact on the mood of your room.

Wallpaper Color Rules of Thumb

• Darker colors will create a warmer, cozier mood, and can make a room seem smaller.

• Lighter colors will create a more contemporary and energizing atmosphere, and can make a room seem bigger and more open.

• Cool colors without a lot of contrast and soft, subtle patterns will give a room a peaceful quality.

• Earth tones, especially in papers featuring simple patterns and textures, give a room a feeling of natural warmth.

• Rich-colored papers and papers with dark accents make a setting seem more formal.

Wallpapers that mimic the look of labor-intensive painting techniques not only cut down on effort, they eliminate the anxiety of the unknown. You don't have to splatter, sponge, or otherwise decorate a wall in paint and glaze to find out if you like a look. These subtly textured strips of paper show you exactly what you'll end up with before you start.

light reflective

These new metallic designs—available in a range of silvers, golds, bronzes, and coppers—provide some of the sharpest, freshest looks in modern wallpapers. They add detail and richness to a room without relying on overpowering colors or overly busy patterns.

pairing papers

One of the most interesting ways to add character to a room is to combine a couple of like-minded wallpapers. Follow these tips for effectively putting papers together.

• One of the easiest approaches is to choose two papers that are similar in both color scheme and design.

• An alternative to choosing two similar papers is to effectively balance two different ones. For example, you might use a bold floral pattern on one wall; then cover the others with a paper that features a single accent piece from the first paper, such as a leaf or a vine.

• If you're using papers that differ, put the one with the larger pattern on the room's focal-point wall—the wall you first see when you enter the room or the wall that frames the room's main feature, such as a fireplace. Use the paper with the subtler pattern on the other walls, to help keep everything in proportion.

• Use a chair rail, a shelf, or some other feature to divide your two papers. Again, if your papers aren't similar in color and pattern size, use the one with the heavier color or pattern on the bottom and the lighter design on top. Otherwise, your room will feel as if it's caving in.

Designed to reflect and refract the light when it hits their surface, these papers can enrich the atmosphere of any room. Some are created with foil or metallic inks. Others get their lustre from mica. Almost all strike a balance between shiny areas and a matt ground. Sunlight, candlelight, and artificial light will all interact differently with light-reflective wallpaper.

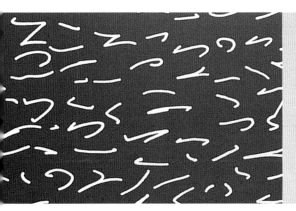

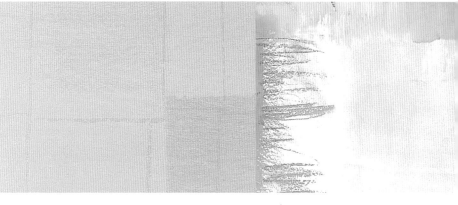

novelty

Nothing offers a solution to the dilemma of plain white walls like the vast array of new novelty papers now on the market. Use them for touches of frivolity, dashes of surprise, and bits of boisterous fun.

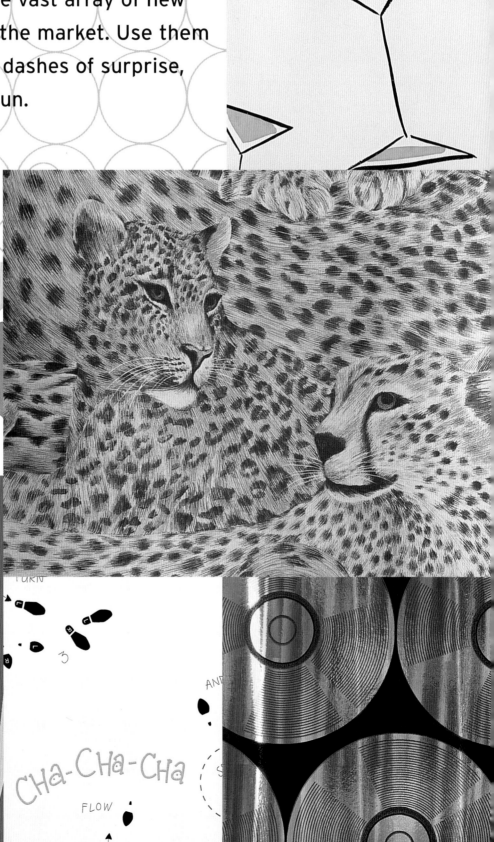

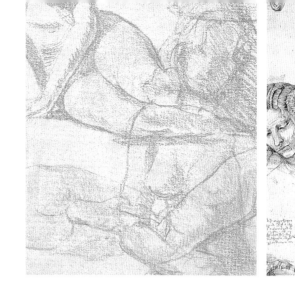

combining surfaces

Papering just one or two walls is often the best way to work a more elaborate wallpaper into a room.

• Assess the room's other wall surfaces. The material you have to coordinate with might be anything from painted plaster or bead-board paneling to exposed brick or concrete.

• Choose your paper to blend with—or provide a dramatic contrast to—the room's other walls.

• Make the one wall you paper the room's focal-point wall—the one surrounding the fireplace or holding the huge mirror, for example.

• If you're using your paper in small doses, it may work to highlight not only a wall but also another piece or two in the room, perhaps the back of a shelf or a set of storage boxes stacked in the corner. For ideas and steps on how to paper objects other than walls, see Wallpaper Accents, page 90.

Whether you want martini olives sprinkled along your sink's back-splash or sunfish darting across a bathroom wall, novelty papers are a perfect way to play up a room's theme—or infuse it with your own personality. They work especially well in kids' rooms and play rooms. They're also just right for unexpected accents in utilitarian spaces, from laundry rooms to pantries.

chapter 2

wallpapering basics

WALLPAPERING HAS THE REPUTATION OF BEING ONE OF THE MORE DEMANDING HOME-DECORATING ENDEAVORS. WHILE IT'S TRUE THAT IT'S MORE INVOLVED THAN ROLLING ON A COAT OF PAINT, WITH THE RIGHT TOOLS AND SOME SIMPLE TECHNIQUES, IT'S NOTHING YOU CAN'T GET THE HANG OF.

how much

Wallpaper comes in different widths and lengths, depending on the style and manufacturer. Here's an easy formula for figuring how much you need of the paper you've chosen.

1. Measure the width of each wall you want to cover, and add the widths together. Round up to the nearest 6 inches (15.2 cm).

2. Multiply the total by the height of the room. Again, round up to the nearest 6 inches (15.2 cm). Go ahead and deduct the measurements of baseboards and crown moldings, but don't worry about deducting the space taken up by windows and doors unless they add up to more than 100 square feet (9 square m). You now have the square footage of the wall space you want to paper.

3. Check the label on the wallpaper you've chosen. It will tell you how many square feet one roll covers. Divide the square footage of the room by the square footage of one roll of paper. The result is the number of rolls you need, but buy at least 10 percent more, so you have extra for errors and adjustments. Match the dye-lot numbers on each roll to avoid slight color differences.

wallpaper tools & supplies

Level. When you need to determine a straight vertical or horizontal line on your walls, use a level.

Paperhanging brush. The flexible bristles help you smooth your hung paper so it's free of bubbles and wrinkles. Instead, you can use a dry, soft sponge or a plastic smoother tool.

Pasting brush (about 4 inches [10.2 cm]) or a **paint roller and tray.** These tools are for applying the paste to the back of the wallpaper.

Plumb line. Simply a weight attached to the end of a string, this tool helps you establish a straight, vertical layout line. Tack the string at the top of the wall so the weight is just above the floor. When the line stops swinging, align a ruler with the string to mark your layout line.

Ruler or yardstick. You'll use it for marking your plumb line.

Scissors. Long-bladed scissors are best for cutting your wallpaper strips to size.

Seam roller. A seam roller is indispensable when it comes to pressing down the seams where two pieces of wallpaper meet, called the join.

Smoother. This flat, plastic tool works much like a paperhanging brush.

Sponge and **pail of water.** You'll use these as you hang your paper to remove any wallpaper paste oozing from the edges of your newly applied paper.

Stepladder. This obvious necessity helps when you're papering from floor to ceiling.

Tape measure. When you're measuring your room dimensions and cutting your paper, you've got to have one. A yardstick will do as a substitute.

Trim guide. A painting edger or a broad knife can serve as a trim guide.

You'll use it to press your wet wallpaper into a ceiling, wall joint, the edges of moldings, or baseboards before you trim it.

Utility knife. Use a knife with breakaway blades in conjunction with your trim guide to cut away excess paper.

Wallpaper paste. If your paper isn't prepasted, you'll need to coat each strip with premixed paste. Use heavy-weight paste for heavier and embossed papers.

Wallpaper sizing. This premixed liquid prepares your walls so you can more easily slide your paper into place. It also works as a good bonding agent.

Water tray. If you're using prepasted wallpaper, you'll need to soak it before hanging it.

Worktable. You want a surface that's at least 5 feet (152.4 cm) long on which you can cut and drip the occasional drop of paste.

TIP: If your paper features a large pattern you're matching from wallpaper strip to wallpaper strip, you'll have to move the strips up and down quite a bit as you work. This causes a lot of waste, so you may want to purchase a roll or two more than the formula on page 36 tells you that you need. If you go back to purchase more later, the new roll may have a different dye-lot number, so your colors might not match perfectly. If you have leftover unopened rolls of paper when you finish, you can always return them.

GO FIGURE: Nobody knows why, but although wallpaper is priced by the single roll, it's often sold only in packages of double rolls—a good thing to keep in mind when you're estimating how much you need to buy.

prep your walls

Give your walls a good washing down and dry them well; then patch any holes or cracks with wall compound. After the compound is dry, sand the patched areas until they're smooth. Also, remove the covers on electrical receptacles and light switches, cover electrical outlets with masking tape, and remove any heating grates or plate covers from your walls. Primer is a *must* only if you're papering over new drywall, but it'll promote adhesion on any type of wall. Finally, apply a coat of wallpaper sizing, and let it dry about an hour.

hang the paper

1. Measure the width of your wallpaper. Then, measure from your starting point out 2 inches (5.1 cm) less than the width of your paper, and drop a plumb line. Mark the line on the wall with a pencil. Measure this vertical line (which is the height of the walls), and add 2 inches (5.1 cm) for the ceiling overlap and 2 inches (5.1 cm) for the baseboard overlap. Cut a wallpaper strip that matches your measurement. If your paper has a pattern, make sure you cut so you'll have a full pattern motif at the ceiling line.

TRIMMING SELVAGES

Some papers come with a blank selvage on each edge. It protects the printed area of the roll during shipping. Use a straight-edge and a utility knife to trim the selvages off before you start papering. Or, avoid this step altogether by making sure you order pretrimmed paper.

2. To cut the next strip, which will adjoin the first, match the pattern across the join, and cut your second strip with a 2-inch (5.1 cm) excess at each end. Sometimes, a wallpaper's pattern will require that you match specific sides of the stripes, which will affect which way you work around a room. To avoid having too many strips lying around (which can cause confusion about which is the second, which is the third, and so on), cut only two at a time. After you hang your first strip, use the second strip to match and cut a third one, then continue working in this way.

TIPS:

• As you cut your strips, mark the tops with a light pencil mark on the back, so you don't accidentally hang them upside down.

• Easy start: If you're tackling one of your first papering projects, wallpapers that feature stripes and small, all-over designs are the easiest to match.

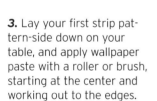

3. Lay your first strip pattern-side down on your table, and apply wallpaper paste with a roller or brush, starting at the center and working out to the edges.

4. Apply paste to as much of the strip as you can fit on the table, then fold that section of the strip neatly in half, with the pasted sides together. Slide the section so it overhangs the table edge, then repeat the process to paste the rest of the strip. Folding the ends in to the center, pasted sides together, is called *booking*.

Prepasted Variation: If your wallpaper is prepasted, fill a water tray half full of lukewarm water.

Roll your strip loosely, pattern side in, for about a minute. Holding one edge of the strip with both hands, lift it out, and make sure the pasted side has been evenly soaked. Fold or book both ends of the strip into the center, pasted sides in.

5. Unfold the upper section of the strip. Hold it between your fingers and thumb, and position it to overlap the ceiling by 2 inches (5.1 cm), aligning it with the penciled vertical guide.

6. From the top, smooth the paper out from the center to the edges. If it's not properly aligned, pull it away and reposition it.

TIP: After pasting a strip, wipe any paste from the table before preparing another strip.

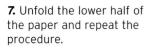

WHERE TO START

If your paper features a large pattern, center your first strip at a focal point in the room, and paper out from that point in each direction. Your goal is to join the last two strips in an inconspicuous corner. With any other wallpaper, start in an inconspicuous corner and work all the way around the room. See figure 1.

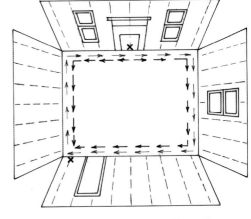

figure 1

7. Unfold the lower half of the paper and repeat the procedure.

8. With the trim guide, hold the paper against the ceiling or molding, and cut away the excess with the utility knife.

9. Remove excess paste with a damp sponge. Repeat, and trim away the excess wallpaper at the baseboard.

10. Continue with the next strip of paper, matching the pattern and butting the edges, using your palm to slide it into place.

11. After 30 minutes, roll the seams gently with a seam roller.

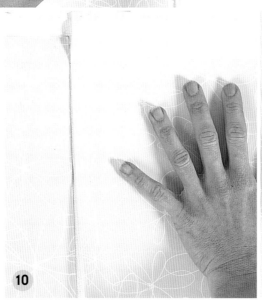

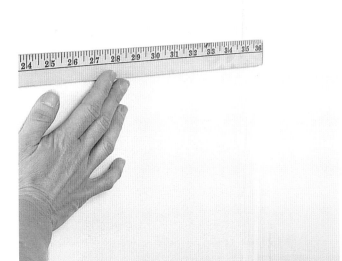

1

corners

If you simply press paper into place in a corner, it will eventually pull away. Instead, follow these steps for a snug and lasting fit.

1. Measure from the last strip before the corner to the corner. Add ½ inch (1.3 cm), and cut to shorten the width of your corner strip to match the measurement.

2. Paste and apply the paper, then use the paper-hanging brush to fit it into the corner.

3. Hold up the leftover portion of the strip you cut in step 1, and mark that distance from the corner. Hang a plumb line from this point and mark it on the wall.

4. Paste and apply the wallpaper from the corner, overlapping the previous strip's extra ½ inch (1.3 cm). Any slight mismatch of pattern here will not be obvious.

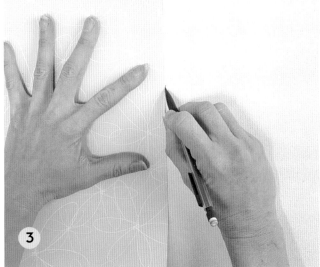

3

2

Tip: Make a small slit at the top and bottom of the paper where it goes into the corner, to help it fit into place.

4

windows and doors

1. Position a wallpaper strip on the wall, so it runs over the door or window casing. Smooth the paper and press the strip tightly against the casing.

2. Cut from the strip's edge to the corner of the casing. Trim away the excess, leaving about 1 inch (2.5 cm) around the inside of the frame.

3. With a trim guide, hold the wallpaper against the casing and trim it with a utility knife. Cut short strips for sections above doors and below windows. Hang them exactly vertical, so you'll be sure to have a pattern match at the next full strip. Apply the next full strip with the edge butting the short one. Snip the corners and trim the excess paper to 1 inch (2.5 cm) around the inside of the frame. On windows, match the seam on the bottom and trim the excess at the window frame's bottom edge to 1 inch (2.5 cm). Use the trim guide to hold the paper against the casing, and cut the excess.

Tip: Remove excess paste from casings and wallpaper with a damp sponge.

Tip: Check any scraps you have to see if they may be what you need for the areas above doors and above and below windows.

switches and outlets

Turn the power off and remove your switch and outlet covers before you start.

1. Hang the paper over the light switches and outlets.

2. Using a utility knife, make small diagonal cuts to expose the switch or outlet.

3. Press the flaps back to the edges, and trim them.

Tip: If necessary, apply extra paste under the edges of a strip of wallpaper to make it lie flat.

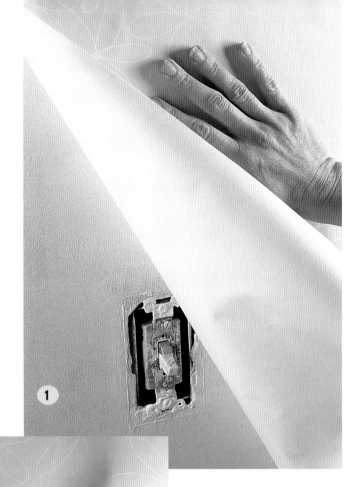

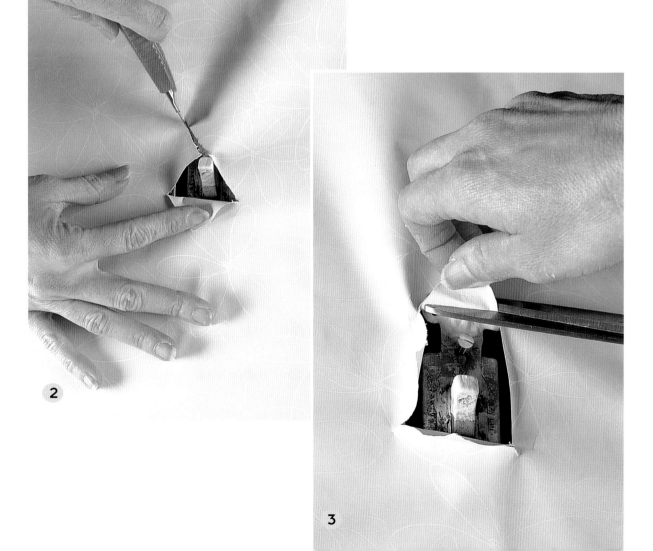

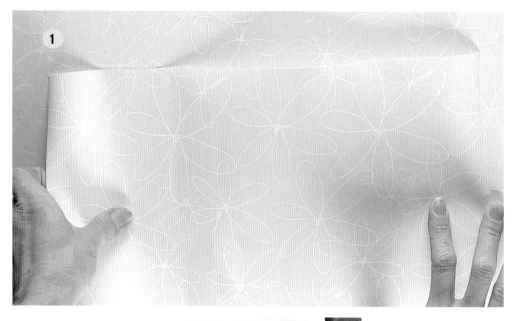

switch and outlet covers

1. Remove the cover and reinsert the screws in the outlet. Find a scrap of wallpaper that matches the area around the outlet. Fasten it over the outlet with low-tack tape to match the pattern.

2. Mark the center of the scrap if you're covering a switch. If you're covering an outlet, hold the paper over the plugs and emboss the surface, then remove the paper and mark the embossed points (where the plugs will be) on the back side of the paper. Lay the cover on the back of the paper, so the hole marks line up.

3. Mark the corners.

4. Trim the scrap ¼ inch (6 mm) wider than the cover.

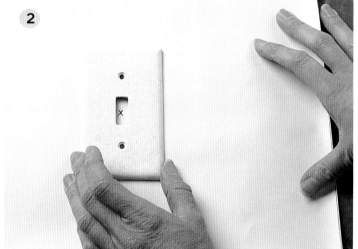

Tip: In bathrooms and bedrooms, consider installing switches with illuminated levers.

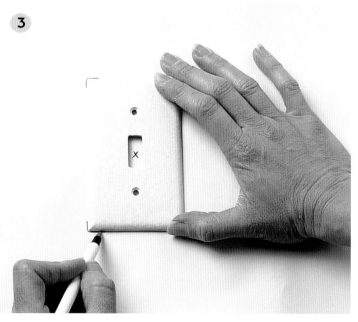

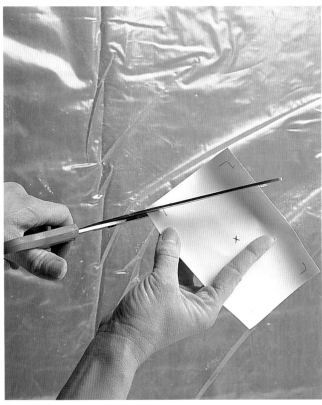

5. Trim the corners. Brush vinyl-on-vinyl adhesive to both the paper and the cover. Attach the paper and smooth it.

6. Wrap the overlap around the back. Secure it with tape.

7. Cut the openings in the cover plate with a utility knife.

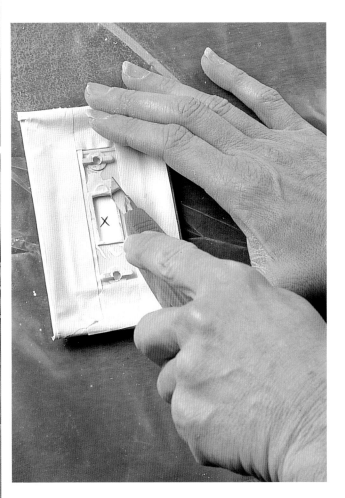

Tip: Look for a vinyl-on-vinyl adhesive in the wallpaper section of home and hardware stores.

chapter 3

walls, ceilings & borders

walls

patchwork walls

Designer: Lyna Farkas

How to choose from the pinstripes, the polka dots, or the subtle paisley pattern? Go ahead and use them all to create a colorful quilt on your wall.

What You Need

8 to 12 wallpapers with patterns and colors that work well together (Purchasing discontinued rolls on sale is a good way to come up with the paper you need for this project. You can also order sample sheets of wallpaper from many wallpaper stores for a nominal cost.)

Wallpaper paste

Cutting mat or something to protect your cutting surface

Utility knife

Ruler

Tape measure

Square ruler

Paste brush

Sponge

Pail of water

Trim guide

What You Do

1. Cut out 1-inch (2.5 cm) squares from each wallpaper, and move them around on a flat surface to come up with the pattern you want to put on your walls.

2. To determine the size of the wallpaper patches you'll need, measure the length and height of each wall, and find a common denominator. For example, a wall that's 12 feet (360 cm) long by 8 feet (240 cm) high can accommodate 8-inch (20.3 cm) squares evenly.

3. Use the square ruler to measure out your patches. Add 1 inch (2.54 cm) to the height of the patches to be on the bottom row, so you'll be sure to have enough coverage. Cut out the patches with the utility knife.

4. Using the pattern you created in step 1 as a guide, brush paste on the back of the first wallpaper patch, and apply it in the upper corner of the wall. Use the sponge to smooth out any excess paste.

5. Apply the next patch, working down. Slightly overlap the patches to allow for shrinkage.

6. When you apply the bottom patches, trim their bottom edges with the trim guide and the utility knife, if necessary.

tattered stripes

Designer: Lyna Farkas

GIVE A ROOM THE BOLDNESS OF STRIPES WITHOUT THEIR USUAL RIGID STRUCTURE. WHEN
YOU CREATE YOUR OWN WIDE, HAND-TORN BANDS LIKE THESE, YOU CAN ALSO ALTERNATE
WALLPAPER COLORS AND EVEN PATTERNS.

What You Need

Satin latex paint (optional)

Wallpaper (You can use just one paper or use two or more that work well together.)

Wallpaper paste

Roller tray and roller with ¼-inch (6 mm) nap (optional)

Tape measure

Scissors

Yardstick

Level

Pasting brush

Sponge

Pail of water

Utility knife

Trim guide

What You Do

1. If you need to change the color of your wall so it better coordinates with your paper, use the roller and paint to do so. Let the wall dry.

2. Decide the width you'd like your wallpaper stripes to be. For example, if your wallpaper is 27 inches (68.6 cm) wide, you can rip three stripes of 7 to 10 inches (17.8 to 25.4 cm) per roll. Also, determine how wide you want the spaces between the stripes.

3. Measure your wall horizontally, add 4 inches (10.2 cm), and cut a strip of wallpaper to length.

4. Place the strip on a table, place the yardstick where you want the edge of your first torn stripe, and slowly tear out the stripe.

5. Continue cutting strips and ripping them, until you have as many torn stripes as you need. Allow the width to vary slightly from stripe to stripe for interest.

6. With the yardstick and the level, mark the placements of your stripes on the wall. Do this by drawing a line all the way across where you want the middle of each stripe.

7. Paste the first stripe and accordion pleat it (see page 60). Apply it, using your first line as a guide. Let the ends extend 2 inches (5.1 cm). Smooth out the stripe with a damp sponge.

8. Continue applying the torn stripes, using your marked lines as guides, and alternating papers according to the design you have in mind.

9. Use the trim guide and utility knife to trim the excess paper from the ends at the corners.

10. Continue around the room, if you plan to paper the whole room, matching paper as best as you can. Let the paper dry overnight.

meeting halfway

Designer: Lyna Farkas

PAPERING JUST ONE SECTION OF A WALL IS A CLASSIC WAY TO
COMBINE WALLPAPER AND PAINT. USE A SHELF, LEDGE, CUPBOARD,
OR CHAIR RAIL AS THE DIVIDING FEATURE, THEN APPLY ONE WALL
TREATMENT ABOVE AND THE OTHER BELOW.

What You Need

Paint (optional)

Wallpaper

Wallpaper paste

Level

Yardstick

Roller tray and ¼-inch (6 mm) nap
roller

Plumb line

Scissors

Pasting brush or roller

Utility knife

Trim guide

Water pail

Sponge

What You Do

1. If you already have a shelf, picture ledge, or other dividing piece in place, remove it from your wall, if possible. Mark a level line from one end of the wall to the other where you want to rehang it. If you can't remove the dividing piece, treat its edges just as you would a baseboard as you work, leaving an overhang of wallpaper you can trim with a trim guide and utility knife (see step 8). If you're starting with a bare wall and plan to install a dividing piece, mark where it will hang with a level line.

2. If you're repainting the wall, use the nap roller to paint from the ceiling to the line you drew in step 1.

3. Measure the width of your paper. Next measure from the corner of the wall out 2 inches (5.1 cm) less than the width of your paper. Hang and mark a plumb line. (If you're papering only this wall and not the adjoining walls, instead of measuring out 2 inches [5.1 cm] less than the width of your paper, measure out ½ inch [1.3 cm] less. This will leave you with less of an amount of excess paper at the corners, and you can simply trim it off in step 7.)

4. Measure the first strip of wallpaper to be hung from the paint line to the baseboard, leaving a 2-inch (5.1 cm) overhang at the baseboard. Cut the strip.

5. Cut the next strip, matching the pattern across the join with the first one.

6. Paste the back of the first section of paper.

7. Butt the edge of the first section of paper to the plumb line and the top of the section to the paint line. Continue to cut strips and apply paper, as described in Wallpapering Basics, page 36, until the wall is complete. If you're papering the adjoining walls in the room, use the steps in Wallpapering Basics for papering around the corners and continuing on around the rest of the room. If you're papering only this wall, use the trim guide and utility knife to trim the paper at the corners.

8. Using the trim guide and the utility knife, trim the wallpaper at the baseboard.

9. Install your shelf or other dividing piece so it covers the overlap of paint and wallpaper.

What You Need

Wallpaper with a solid or simple texture that coordinates with the wallpaper you plan to cut into shapes (Optional. You don't have to paper your walls first; this technique works just as well on painted walls.)

A bolder wallpaper for your shapes (Here, we used silver metallic paper.)

Poster board at least 20 inches (50.8 cm) wide

Ellipse pattern, page 124 (Optional. Choose another shape, if you like.)

Wallpaper paste

Scissors

Straightedge

Craft knife

Level

Pasting brush

Sponge

Pail of water

Plumb line

Utility knife

Trim guide

wallpaper shapes

Designer: Lyna Farkas

JUST BECAUSE WALLPAPER COMES IN NICE, SOLID STRIPS DOESN'T MEAN YOU HAVE TO USE IT THAT WAY. ALL YOU NEED IS A TEMPLATE TO CUT THOSE STRIPS INTO OVALS, CIRCLES, OR ANY SHAPE YOU LIKE. THEN YOU CAN PASTE THEM IN PLACE WHEREVER YOU PLEASE.

What You Do

1. If you're papering your walls to start with, do so following the techniques in Wallpapering Basics, page 36.

2. Determine your design, deciding where you want to place ellipses (or other shapes) and vertical stripes. Consider having your shapes wrap around corners and straddle angles.

3. Enlarge the ellipse pattern, page 124, to the size you want, or choose another shape. Trace it onto poster board to make a template.

4. Use the poster-board template to cut the number of ellipses you need from the bolder wallpaper.

5. With the straightedge and the craft knife, cut the number of vertical stripes you need, making

them 3 inches (7.6 cm) wide and 4 inches (10.2 cm) longer then the height of the walls.

6. Use the ellipse template to pencil in where you want ellipses on the wall, checking each with the level as you do.

7. One at a time, paste the back of each ellipse, place it on the wall using the penciled guide, smooth it in place, and remove

any excess paste with a damp sponge.

8. To position each stripe, mark a vertical plumb line on the wall.

9. One at a time, paste each stripe and book it to make it easier to handle. Align it with one side of the plumb line, and begin positioning it at the ceiling, leaving a 2-inch (5.1 cm) overlap at the ceiling line. Smooth the stripe with the sponge as you work down the wall. Remove all excess paste.

10. Use the utility knife and trim guide to trim the excess paper at the ceiling and baseboard.

cut out & customize

Designer: Sara-Beth Black

This project, perfect for kids' rooms, uses wallpaper that features castles, turrets, and flags. But you could just as easily use flowers, trees, and clouds, or some other themed combination. Simply cut and paste the individual elements to create a wall mural perfectly tailored to your child's room and personality.

What You Need

Castle, turret and flag wallpapers, or wallpapers that feature some other motif

Wallpaper paste

Scissors

Pasting brush

Smoother

What You Do

1. On each wall, sketch the general layout you have in mind.

2. Cut the pieces you'll need for the first wall, trimming around the imagery and cutting out details as you like. Vary the heights and widths of the elements you cut out to add diversity to the design.

3. Paste the first cutout piece, and book it (see page 39).

4. Apply the piece to the wall, and smooth it.

5. Continue adding large pieces until you complete the foundation of your "mural" on each wall.

6. One at a time, paste the accent pieces; in this case, they were turrets and flags.

7. Apply the pieces where you want them, butting the edges together when necessary.

molding insert

Designer: Lyna Farkas

ADD THE CHARM OF ARCHITECTURAL DETAIL TO ANY FLAT, ORDI-
NARY WALL. FIRST, PASTE IN PLACE PANELS OF WALLPAPER, THEN
FRAME EACH WITH STRIPS OF PREMADE MOLDING.

What You Need

Butcher paper (optional)

Masking tape (optional)

Wallpaper

Wallpaper paste

Wood molding

Satin latex paint

Finish nails

Caulk

Level

Yardstick

Scissors

Pasting brush

Sponge

Pail of water

Saw

Miter box

Small paintbrush

Drill and ¹⁄₁₆-inch (1.6 mm) bit

Hammer

Nail set

Smoother

What You Do

1. Using the level, mark the position of your molding frame on the wall. You might find it helpful to make false panels with butcher paper and tape them to the wall to get a complete picture of the layout.

2. Cut strips of wallpaper to fill your planned molding frame.

3. Paste and book the paper.

4. Apply the first strip to the wall at the top corner of your frame, and smooth it down to the bottom of the outline. Remove any excess paste with a damp sponge.

5. Apply the next strip, starting at the top and butting the edge to the first strip. Again, remove any excess paste with the sponge. Continue until you've filled the area you want to frame.

6. Use the yardstick to measure your molding strips; then mark 45-degree cutting lines. Use the miter box and saw to cut them. Test-fit the first molding cuts before making the others.

7. Paint the molding strips, and let them dry.

8. Drill holes near the ends of the molding strips.

9. Position the top strip on the wall, over the top edge of the wallpaper. Nail it in place, leaving the nail heads slightly above the surface.

10. Nail the side strips in place, then fit the bottom piece, adjusting it, if necessary, so all the joints fit tightly at the corners.

11. Drive the nails slightly below the surface with the nail set. Fill the holes and the corner joints with caulk, then touch up the areas with paint.

sideways stripes

Designer: Lyna Farkas

SOME WALLPAPERS, LIKE THIS ONE FEATURING VIVID STRIPES, LOOK AS GREAT RUNNING SIDEWAYS AS THEY DO STRAIGHT UP AND DOWN. ONE OF THE EASIEST WAYS TO ACHIEVE A DRAMATIC EFFECT IS TO APPLY A SINGLE, HORIZONTAL STRIP BELOW A LOW CHAIR RAIL OR SHELF.

What You Need

Wallpaper

Wallpaper paste

Tape measure

Level

Roller tray and ¼-inch (6 mm) nap roller

Plumb line

Scissors

Pasting brush

Water pail

Sponge

Utility knife

What You Do

1. To hang a single strip of paper horizontally, measure the width of the strip, transfer the measurement to the wall (measuring up from where the wall meets the floor or the baseboard), and mark a level line along the wall.

2. Measure the wall horizontally, add 4 inches (10.2 cm), and cut your strip of wallpaper to match the measurement.

3. Paste the back of the strip and apply it, letting the paper extend 2 inches (5.1 cm) at each wall edge or corner. Smooth the strip with a wet sponge and remove any excess paste.

4. Apply single strips to the room's other walls. To butt them together, lap each continuing strip over the one next to it by about ½ inch (1.3 cm). Make a cut through both layers with the utility knife and remove the excess wallpaper, and you'll be left with two strips that butt perfectly (see figure 1).

5. Install a shelf, chair rail, or other dividing piece above the strip, if you like.

VARIATION: If you want several horizontal strips stacked on top of each other, begin by marking a level line on the wall where you want the wallpaper to start. Align your first strip with the line, then apply your second one below it, butting it neatly against the first.

Tip: See the project on page 52 for details about papering underneath an existing shelf, a chair rail, or another dividing piece.

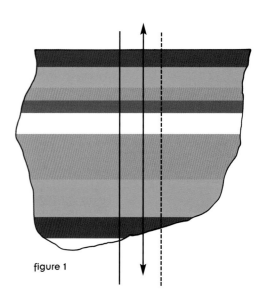

figure 1

ceilings

ceilings basics

Whether you want to hide cracks and other imperfections or add interest to a room, papering your ceiling can do the trick. Here are the basics for covering your ceiling completely with paper. In this section, we also show you some even easier ways to add wallpaper accents overhead.

how much

Use this simple formula to decide how much wallpaper you need to cover a ceiling.

Width of room ÷ wallpaper width = A

Length of room x A = B

B ÷ length of a roll of the wallpaper you've selected = number of rolls you need

hanging

1. Mark a guide on your ceiling for hanging your first strip of wallpaper. Measure the width of the wallpaper strip, and subtract $1/2$ inch (1.3 cm). Measure this distance away from the wall edge at several intervals, and mark the points on the ceiling. Using a straight-edge, draw a line along the points.

2. Cut your first two strips of wallpaper, matching the pattern, if necessary. Make the strips 4 inches (10.2 cm) longer than your ceiling length. As you continue to work, use the strip you're preparing to hang to cut the next one, just as you would for papering walls. The idea is not to have too many strips lying around at once.

3. Paste the first strip and fold it back and forth, accordion style, with the pasted side in (see figure 1). This will make it easier to handle when you begin applying it to the ceiling.

figure 1

4. Apply the first strip against the guide line. You'll have a $1/2$-inch (1.3 cm) overlap along the side wall and a 2-inch (5.1 cm) overlap at both end walls.

5. Smooth the strip with a brush, starting at the center and working out.

6. Trim the edge and the ends with a trim guide and utility knife. If you'll be papering the walls, trim the ceiling overlap to $1/2$ inch (1.3 cm).

TIPS:

• It's a good idea to make a mini scaffold by placing a sturdy board between two ladders. This will allow you to easily get from one end of the ceiling to the other.

• If you don't have a partner to help you, use the handle of a broom to press the accordion-booked end of your wallpaper strip to the ceiling until you're ready to continue unfolding it.

• If you're papering both the walls and ceiling, apply the ceiling paper first. Remember, the ceiling pattern can blend perfectly with only one wall.

• When papering a ceiling, begin hanging your strips at the far end of the room, or whichever end is more visible. Also, work across the width of the ceiling, so you have shorter strips to hang.

7. Cut a diagonal in the overlap at the corners, so the strip will lie flat. Press the paper into the corners.

8. Continue hanging the rest of the strips, butting their edges.

papering around ceiling fixtures

If there's a fixture on the ceiling, turn off the electricity and remove the light bulb and fixture. Unscrew the cover to disconnect the wires, and then replace the cover plate to protect the wires from the wet paste.

Tip: Make a color drawing of the wiring before you disconnect it to use as a guide for rewiring when you're finished.

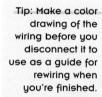

figure 2

1. Paper the ceiling up to the cover plate, pressing the paper lightly over the plate. Pierce the paper with a sharp pair of scissors in the middle top part of the cover plate.

2. Make several slits outward from the hole to reveal the cover plate. Loosen the cover and trim the paper slits until they're short enough to brush onto the ceiling, under the cover (see figure 2).

3. Continue hanging the length of paper.

rose ceiling

Designer: Lyna Farkas

WE MADE OUR OWN CEILING MEDALLION AND ADDED A BORDER FROM THE SAME FLORAL PAPER FOR A SOFT, ROMANTIC LOOK. CREATE A SIMILAR EFFECT WITH ANY PAPER FEATURING LARGE BLOOMS.

What You Need

Wallpaper with a large rose or floral motif

Wallpaper paste

Compass

Scissors

Paste brush

Sponge

Pail of water

Utility knife

Straightedge

Seam roller

What You Do

1. Use the compass to lightly mark a circle on the back of the wallpaper. The size of the circle will depend on the size and shape of the light fixture you want it to work with.

2. Cut out the circle, adapting the edges to the shapes of the flowers.

3. Find the center of the medallion, and mark it lightly.

4. Remove your light fixture.

5. Brush paste on the back of the medallion and apply it to the ceiling, lining up the center of the medallion and the middle of the fixture area.

6. Press the medallion with a damp sponge and remove the excess paste. Once the paper dries, reinstall the light fixture. You may need to make a small cutout in the center of the medallion to do so.

7. Measure the four sides of the ceiling, add 4 inches (10.2 cm) to each measurement, and cut four strips of wallpaper. Make each strip about 10 inches (25.4 cm) wide, and use the scissors to adapt the edges to the shapes of the flowers, as you did on the medallion.

8. Paste the first strip and accordion pleat it.

9. Apply the strip, beginning at one corner and following the edge. Smooth it with a damp sponge and remove the excess paste.

10. Paste and apply the next strip in the same way, on a perpendicular edge.

11. To miter the corner, hold the straightedge along the intersection of the points of paper at the corner. Cut through both layers with the utility knife (see figure 1). Peel back the strips and remove the cut ends. Press the paper back in place.

12. Paper the other edges, mitering the corners as you go.

13. After 30 minutes, use the seam roller to press the corners.

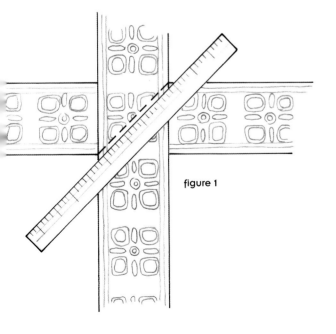

figure 1

spiral ceiling treatment

Designer: Lyna Farkas

IF YOU HAVE A KID'S ROOM, A PLAY ROOM, OR SOME OTHER SPACE THAT NEEDS A LITTLE PERKING UP, THIS SIMPLEST OF CEILING APPLICATIONS WILL DO IT. WITH ALL THE NEW NOVELTY PAPERS AVAILABLE TODAY, YOUR SPIRAL COULD FEATURE ANYTHING FROM PLANETS AND CLOUDS TO FROGS AND FISH.

What You Need

Wallpaper with a continuous pattern of a simple shape

Wallpaper paste

Utility knife or craft knife

Paste brush

Sponge

Pail of water

What You Do

1. Use the utility or craft knife to carefully cut out the shapes from the wallpaper.

2. Lightly draw out your spiral on the ceiling. You can create one central spiral emanating from a light fixture, as we did here, or create smaller spirals all over the ceiling.

3. Paste the back of the first shape and apply it, then press on the center of the spiral with a damp sponge to remove any excess paste.

4. Paste and apply the second shape about an inch (2.5 cm) away from the first shape on the spiral line.

5. Continue with each shape, distancing them a bit more as the spiral gets bigger.

TIP: To check the spacing of your spiral, tape each piece in place first and make sure you're happy with the look before you paste.

tiled ceiling

Designer: Lyna Farkas

IT'S AMAZING HOW AN EMBOSSED WALLPAPER AND A BIT OF GLAZE OR PAINT CAN TRANSFORM EVEN A BRAND NEW CEILING INTO ONE THAT LOOKS HISTORIC. THIS LOOK IS ESPECIALLY GOOD FOR HIGH CEILINGS.

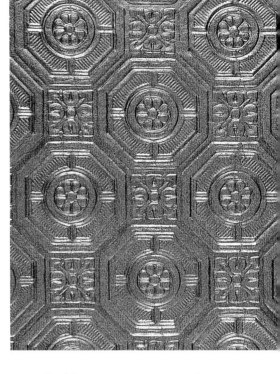

glaze-and-wipe technique for an antiqued look

What You Need

Embossed wallpaper

Heavy-duty wallpaper paste

White paint

Painter's tube of acrylic raw umber

Glaze

Tape measure

Utility knife

Straightedge

4-inch (10.2 cm) pasting brush

Sponge

Pail of water

Roller and tray

3-inch (7.6 cm) brush

Mixing bowl

Damp lint-free rag

What You Do

1. Paper your ceiling, following the steps on page 60.

2. Roll two coats of paint onto the papered ceiling. It may be necessary to pounce paint into the paper's crevices with a brush.

3. Mix one part of raw umber paint to two parts glaze in the bowl.

4. Apply the glaze with the brush, working on sections about 2 feet by 2 feet (61 x 61 cm). Pounce the glaze into the crevices.

5. Bunch the damp rag to form a puff, and swirl it around on the paper's surface to wipe off the glaze. The glaze will remain in the crevices, accenting the embossed pattern. Work fast to be sure the edges of the section don't dry. Your goal is a nice, even look.

6. Continue glazing and wiping the entire ceiling.

variation: papered "tin" ceiling

For this version, you need embossed paper featuring a tile pattern or one similar to an old tin ceiling and some metallic copper spray paint.

1. Measure the length and width of your ceiling to determine how many strips of wallpaper you'll need. In this case, cut all your strips at once, being sure to match the patterns on adjoining strips before you cut them.

2. Take the strips outside or to a well-ventilated area, and spray them with the metallic copper paint until they're well covered. Let them dry.

3. Following the instructions on papering a ceiling, page 60, apply the paper. With embossed paper, butt the first strip as close to the ceiling edge as possible, and butt each strip edge as you apply it. To avoid damaging embossed paper, don't press the edges too hard as you apply it, and use extra care when pressing out excess glue with the sponge.

borders

Not ready to tackle an entire wall? Hanging a border is an excellent and easy way to test your interest in wallpapering—and it may add all the decorative accent you need. Borders come in all kinds of patterns and various widths for hanging around windows, doors, mirrors, and along the tops of walls. You can also pair borders with papers, treating the borders as dividers and frames.

chair rail

A WALLPAPER BORDER AS A CHAIR RAIL CAN HELP LINK TWO DIFFERENT PAPERS—ONE ABOVE AND ONE BELOW—OR PROVIDE A BREAK AND SOME INTEREST ON A FULLY PAPERED WALL.

What You Need

Wallpapers and border

Wallpaper paste

Border paste

Yardstick

Level

Scissors

Paste brush

Roller and tray

Smoother

Sponge

Pail of water

Trim guide

Utility knife

Straightedge

project 1: two different papers with border as chair rail

What You Do

1. Measure your wall from the floor to where you want your chair rail (about 34 inches [86.4 cm] is standard). Using the level and a pencil, lightly mark a line around the room at this height.

2. Prepare and hang the upper wallpaper from the ceiling to the line, using the steps shown in Wallpapering Basics, page 36.

3. Prepare and hang the bottom paper directly under the top paper, butting the edges. Let everything set overnight.

4. Hold the border to the wall so the middle aligns with the point where the two papers join. Mark a short line at the bottom of the border.

5. Using the level and a pencil, lightly extend the line around the room.

6. Identify the least noticeable corner in the room. Measure one of the adjoining walls, and cut the first strip of border so it just goes around the corner of it.

7. Apply border paste down the center and spread it out thinly and evenly toward the edges of the border, covering the edges well.

8. Accordion pleat the border (see page 60), and apply it.

9. Cut and prepare the second strip, and place it slightly over the end of the first, matching the pattern. Lay a straight-edge over the borders at the overlap, and cut through both layers with a utility knife. Peel away the waste and smooth down the ends to form a perfectly butted join (refer back to figure 1, page 59).

10. Continue applying border strips around the room. When you return to the starting point, use the straightedge and utility knife to create another perfect join, as described in step 9.

VARIATION

Instead of using two different papers, use the basic steps for covering your wall with just one paper, then add a chair-rail border as an accent. Or, wallpaper the top portion of your wall only, paint the wall below, and add a border in between.

project 2: using a border as a frame

USE HORIZONTAL AND VERTICAL STRIPS TO FRAME A SINGLE WALL PANEL, FROM CHAIR RAIL TO CEILING.

What You Do

1. Paper your wall as described in Project 1, using two different papers that meet at chair-rail height.

2. Following the steps in Project 1, apply your wallpaper border chair rail.

3. Measure from the ceiling to your chair-rail line, and cut a strip of border to match the length, with a 2-inch (5.1 cm) overhang at each end.

4. Apply border paste down the center and spread it out thinly and evenly toward the edges of the border, covering the edges well. Accordion fold the strip.

5. Place the strip over the wallpaper at the corner of the wall or at the window trim or door trim. Press it and smooth it down.

6. Miter the corner where the borders meet in a perpendicular. To do so, hold the straightedge along the intersection points of paper at the corner. Cut through both layers with the utility knife (refer back to figure 1, page 62). Peel back the strips and remove the cut ends. Press the paper back in place.

7. Continue to make your frame by applying a horizontal piece at the ceiling line and another vertical strip on the opposite edge of the framed area, again mitering the corners.

handmade borders

Designer: Lyna Farkas

THESE FIVE PROJECTS OFFER CREATIVE WAYS TO DECORATE YOUR OWN BORDERS TO ADD A PERSONAL TOUCH TO ANY ROOM. SOME WALLPAPER STORES SELL BLANK BORDERS READY TO BE PERSONALIZED. IF YOU CAN'T FIND THEM, YOU CAN ALSO BUY PAPER BORDERS IN THE CLEARANCE SECTION OF A WALLPAPER STORE AND PRIME THEM. CHOOSE THOSE THAT ARE PASTEL, LIGHTLY PATTERNED, AND WITHOUT TEXTURE.

stencilling

What You Need

Primed wallpaper border

Dark blue paint

Star shapes (or whatever shape you choose) to use as templates

Poster board

Spray shellac

White paint

Glitter paint

Nap roller and tray

Craft knife

Cutting pad or a small piece of flat glass

Cosmetic sponge

Paper towels

What You Do

1. Roll blue paint onto the primed border. The first coat should give the border a nice texture, but leave some white showing through like star clusters. Let it dry.

2. Using the templates, cut several different size star stencils out of poster board with the craft knife. Cut on the cutting pad or on a piece of glass.

3. Spray the edges of the star stencils with spray shellac to keep paint from seeping outside the edges.

4. Place one of the stencils on the border. Dab some white paint on the cosmetic sponge, blot the sponge on a paper towel to discharge excess paint, and dab the sponge on the stencil, covering the whole open area.

5. Continue down the length of the border, creatively spacing the different stars.

6. Once the stars are dry, roll the glitter paint over the entire border.

stamping

What You Need

Primed wallpaper border

Metallic craft paints in a variety of golds, bronze, and copper

3-inch (7.6 cm) sponge roller and tray

Sponge stamps of acorns and leaves (or any motif you like)

Cosmetic sponges

What You Do

1. Apply light gold to the border with the sponge roller. Let it dry. Coat it again until you have a nice, solid coat. Let it dry.

2. Apply dark gold or bronze paint to a leaf stamp with a cosmetic sponge.

3. Randomly stamp the border, pressing evenly.

4. Coat other leaf stamps with other colors and continue stamping, leaving spaces for acorn stamps.

5. Apply copper paint to the acorn stamp with a cosmetic sponge. Stamp acorns randomly down the length of the border. Feel free to overlap images and stamp more leaves until you have a design you're pleased with.

paper napkin decoupage

What You Need

Primed border

Colorful paper napkins

Paint to match one of the colors in the napkins

Decoupage medium

Water-based varnish

Sponge roller with tray

1-inch (2.5 cm) brush

What You Do

1. Apply two coats of paint with the roller. Let it dry.

2. Separate your napkins into single layers, and tear them up into small pieces.

3. Brush pieces of napkin to the border with the decoupage medium. Lightly layer them. Continue adding pieces until you're happy with the way the border is covered. Let it cure overnight.

4. Roll a layer of varnish over the border.

photo transfer

Your border needs to be as smooth as possible for this technique. Plain banner paper, available at craft stores, works better than actual wallpaper borders. Simply cut a strip of banner paper to the border width you want.

What You Need

Photographs

Fabric transfer paper

Banner paper

Computer, scanner, and printer

Pillowcase

Flat plastic surface

Iron

Spray varnish

What You Do

1. Scan the photos, and print them out onto the transfer paper.

2. Preheat the iron for eight minutes.

3. Place the pillowcase on the flat surface, and lay the banner paper on top.

4. Place the transfer paper on the banner paper, photo-side down, positioning photos where you want them.

5. Iron slowly over the back of the transfer paper.

6. Lift up a corner of the transfer paper to check whether the photos have transferred. When they have, lift off the transfer paper.

7. Let the border cool, then spray it with varnish.

low-tech variation

Here's how to transfer photos to a border without a computer. Only black-and-white photocopies work with this technique.

What You Do

1. Make enough photocopies of your photos to cover the entire length of the border.

2. Place the first copy facedown on the border.

3. Dampen a cotton ball with some oil of wintergreen, and burnish the back of the copy until the photo transfers to the border.

4. Continue until you've covered your border with photos. Let everything set overnight.

5. Roll some water-based varnish over the border.

freehand design

What You Need

Primed wallpaper border

Paint in a color of your choice

White chalk

White paint, diluted

Sponge roller and tray

Round artist's brush, approximately ½ inch (1.3 cm)

What You Do

1. Roll the paint onto your primed border. Let it dry, then apply a second coat and let it dry.

2. Draw your freehand pattern in chalk. If you like, add swirls, diamonds, stars, and other elements, so you fill the border.

3. Use the round brush to go over the chalk lines with diluted white paint, adding a nice shading effect.

chapter 4
alternative papers

maps

Designers: Lyna Farkas & Terry Taylor

MATCH YOUR MAPS TO THE PERSONALITY OF THE PLACE YOU'RE PAPERING. TRY MAPS OF THE WATER PARK FOR THE KIDS' BATHROOM, TRAIL MAPS FOR THE MUD ROOM WHERE EVERYONE KEEPS THEIR HIKING BOOTS, AND ANTIQUED ROAD MAPS LIKE THESE FOR THE STUDY.

What You Need

Maps

Brewed tea (optional)

Wallpaper paste

Water-based varnish

Small paintbrush (optional)

Paste brush

Sponge

Pail of water

Paint roller and tray

What You Do

1. If you want your maps to look aged, brush some brewed tea over them and let them dry. Add additional coats, if necessary, until they have the patina you want.

2. Tear puzzle-piece shapes, about 24 inches (61 cm) and larger, out of the maps.

3. Apply a patch of paste about 2-feet (61 cm) square to the top corner of the wall.

4. Start with a piece of map that has a straight edge, position it over the pasted area, and brush it into place with the paste brush.

5. Apply the second piece next to the first, overlapping them about $1/2$ inch (1.3 cm). Brush it on with the paste brush. Save the pieces with straight edges for the ceiling, baseboard, and corner lines.

6. Continue until your walls are covered, wiping off the excess paste with the dampened sponge. Let them dry overnight.

7. Roll a coat of water-based varnish over all the papered walls.

VARIATIONS

For different looks with the same basic technique, consider sheets of newspaper, magazine covers, blueprints, or floor plans.

tissue paper

Designer: Lyna Farkas

START WITH WALLS PAINTED WHITE OR PASTEL WITH A SATIN SHEEN. PASTE
ON SHEETS OF CRUMPLED TISSUE, COVER THEM WITH A PEARLESCENT GLAZE,
AND YOU END UP WITH A SOFTLY TEXTURED, LUMINOUS LOOK.

What You Need

Lightweight wallpaper paste

White tissue paper, ripped in
10- to 12-inch (25.4 to 30.5 cm)
sections and crumpled (You'll
probably need about 10 rolls
of tissue paper to paper a
small room.)

Pearlescent or metallic glaze

3-inch (7.6 cm) brush

Sponge

Pail of water

What You Do

1. Starting at the top corner of the wall, brush
paste on a 2-foot (61 cm)
section, and apply a piece
of tissue against the
edge of the wall. Brush it
into position with the
pasted brush. Save the
pieces of tissue with
straight edges for the ceiling, baseboard, and corner
lines. Tear all the way
around the other pieces.

2. Apply a second piece of
tissue, overlapping the
first about ¼ inch (6 mm).

4. Continue applying the
tissue in this way,
working horizontally or
vertically, whichever works
best for you.

5. Once the room is finished, let it dry overnight.

6. To give the walls a
finished look, lightly brush
on a pearlescent or metallic glaze.

VARIATION

Add extra interest to a wall
papered with tissue by incor-
porating small images that
reinforce a design theme or
simply enhance the look. All
you need are photocopies of
your decorative elements. You
can scatter them on the walls
randomly or use them to create a border or chair rail.

1. Brush wallpaper paste on
the back of the
images, and apply them.
Smooth them and remove the
excess paste with a damp
sponge.

2. Apply tissue over the
images to soften their look, or
bunch some tissue around
each to highlight them.

Satin latex paint (optional)

Scrap paper

Postcards or note cards (If you're working with folded note cards, cut off the front of the card, so you have a single-sided image.)

Heavyweight wallpaper paste

Clear varnish

Roller tray and roller with ¼-inch (6 mm) nap (optional)

Level

Paste brush

Seam roller

Sponge

Pail of water

Paint tray

Sponge roller

What You Do

1. If you like, paint your walls a color that accents your cards.

2. Roughly sketch out some groupings for your cards, then lay the cards out according to your sketch. Rearrange them until you're happy with the design.

3. Lightly mark the placement of the groupings on your walls, using the level to make sure they're straight.

4. Paste the backs of the first group of cards. Apply them to the wall, press them in place with the seam roller, and wipe off any excess paste with a damp sponge.

5. Continue the process until you've covered your walls as planned. Let everything dry.

6. Roll on a coat of clear varnish with the sponge roller.

note card clusters

Designers: Lyna Farkas & Terry Taylor

A BATCH OF NOTE CARDS FEATURING ABSTRACT ART, A COLLECTION OF POSTCARDS FROM TRAVELING FRIENDS, ANTIQUE CHRISTMAS CARDS YOU BOUGHT AT A FLEA MARKET—ALL INGREDIENTS FOR ONE-OF-A-KIND PAPER EMBELLISHMENTS FOR YOUR WALLS.

black-and-white montage

Designers: Lyna Farkas & Terry Taylor

CREATE YOUR OWN GRAPHIC WALL MOSAIC WITH PHOTOGRAPHS, IMAGES FROM A WALL CALENDAR, ADS CLIPPED FROM MAGAZINES, OR PAGES OF COPYRIGHT-FREE ART. THE FUN IS IN LAYERING THEM IN PLACE SO THEY INTERACT WITH OTHER ELEMENTS ON THE WALL—FROM SCONCES TO SHELVES—AND WITH THE FURNITURE IN THE ROOM.

What You Need

Black-and-white images

Wallpaper paste

Water-based varnish

Level

3-inch (7.6 cm) pasting brush

Sponge

Pail of water

Paint tray and sponge roller

What You Do

1. Work out your arrangement on a table or on the floor. Overlap the images, and configure them in a rough circle or oval.

2. Decide where on the wall you want your montage. Draw a horizontal level line to use as a guide for placing it.

3. Paste the back of the most central image, apply it to the wall, using the level line as a guide, and press it down with the damp sponge, removing any excess paste.

4. Apply the next image in the same way, overlapping the first and checking it with the level to make sure it's straight. Continue until you've applied the entire arrangement to the wall.

5. Roll on a coat of varnish to protect the images.

joss paper

Designer: Lyna Farkas

ACTUALLY GILDING YOUR WALLS IS A BIT OF AN UNDERTAKING—SEE THE VARIATION ON PAGE 83 IF YOU'RE INTENT ON THE REAL THING. BUT YOU CAN ACHIEVE A SIMILAR EFFECT BY LAYERING GLITTERING SLIPS OF ASIAN JOSS PAPER ON YOUR WALLS. THESE SMALL SECTIONS OF RICE PAPER THAT FEATURE METALLIC LEAF ARE AVAILABLE AT PAPER AND SCRAPBOOKING STORES, ART-SUPPLY STORES, AND ASIAN MARKETS.

What You Need

Sheets of joss paper with a hint of gilding

Latex paint in a color that matches the base color of your joss paper

Wallpaper paste

Paint roller with ¼-inch (6 mm) nap and roller tray

Measuring tape

Plumb line

Pasting brush

Sponge

Pail of water

Level

Trim guide

Utility knife

What You Do

1. Paint the walls you're papering. This will help the small seams—inevitable with paper like this that can be irregular—to be less noticeable.

2. Start at an inconspicuous corner of your room, so if you need to trim the last row when you work your way back around, it won't be noticeable. From the corner, measure out the width of your joss paper. Drop a plumb line and mark it on the wall.

2. Brush paste on the back of a piece of joss paper, and apply it at the top corner of the wall, butting it against the edge of the wall and aligning its outside edge with the plumb line. Press it down with the dampened sponge, wiping off any excess paste.

3. Apply the next piece of joss paper directly below the first, butting the edges together. Continue down the wall, then start a second row at the top,

butting the edge of the first piece in the second row against the first piece in the first row.

4. Continue in this way, using the level to check the straightness of the lines vertically and horizontally as you work.

5. Once you finish the wall, if there's an overhang at the baseboard or an overlap at the corner, trim it with the trim guide and utility knife.

7. If you trimmed an overlap at the corner and you're covering the adjacent wall, you'll want to begin by applying the trimmed pieces. Align each with the cut piece on the first wall and apply it. They'll form the first vertical row on the adjacent wall.

8. Once you've finished all your walls, go back to the first wall. Starting again at the top corner, paste and press a piece of joss paper in the middle of the four papers in the corner. Press it in place and remove any excess paste.

9. Continue this process down and across, so each grouping of four squares has a square overlapping it in the middle.

gilded wall variation

IF YOU HAVE A WALL THAT NEEDS AN ESPECIALLY RICH LOOK, GILD IT WITH SQUARES OF GOLD LEAF.

What You Need

Red latex paint

Oil-based sizing (Unlike water-based sizing, which stays tacky indefinitely,

oil-based sizing stays tacky for up to three hours and then hardens. Because this technique leaves some paint exposed, you need this feature in the sizing.)

Transfer books of gold leaf (These come in 12 to 24 carat. Each leaf is backed with wax paper. To estimate how much you need, figure your room size in square feet. There are typically 25 leaves in a book. Roughly, 16 leaves will cover 1 square foot [30.5 x 30.5 cm].)

Roller tray and ½-inch (1.3 cm) nap roller

3-inch (7.6 cm) paintbrush

Sponge roller

Gilder's mop brush or soft cosmetic brush

Soft, lint-free rag

What You Do

1. Paint your walls with the red paint, using the nap roller. You may need three or four coats for good coverage. Use the brush to cut around the moldings and corners. Let the paint dry for 24 hours.

2. Starting at the wall's top corner, use the sponge roller to apply some sizing

to an area of the wall that covers several square feet. Wait about 15 minutes until it gets tacky.

3. Hold a piece of gold leaf by its wax-paper overhang, and position it at the top corner of the wall. Place the gold side on the wall, and smooth it down with a gilder's mop brush or a cosmetic brush. The wax paper will loosen as the gold sticks to the wall.

4. Place the next leaf beside the first one but not overlapping. You want a bit of the paint to show through between them.

5. Continue until you've covered the sized area. Apply sizing to an adjoining section of the wall, wait for it to get tacky, and continue.

6. When you reach the baseboard, let the excess leaf rest on it until the tack wears off the sizing. Leaving it in place overnight is ideal.

7. The next day, brush over the walls and the baseboard area with a mop brush, catching any loose portions of gold leaf in a can or envelope to use later.

brown paper wrapping

Designer: Jamesa B. Selleck

GIVE YOUR WALLS A RICH, DIMENSIONAL LOOK WITH THE MOST
INEXPENSIVE OF MATERIALS—THE PLAIN BROWN PAPER USED FOR
PARCEL WRAPPING AND GROCERY BAGS. APPLY IT CRUMPLED, AND
YOU ACHIEVE TEXTURE. LAY IT ON FLAT, AND YOUR WALLS WILL
LOOK AS IF THEY'RE COVERED IN LEATHER.

What You Need

Brown craft paper (Buying
rolls of craft paper is the
easiest way to go. You'll
need about 10 rolls to
paper a small room. You
can also use torn paper
bags, freezer paper, or
resin paper.)

Wallpaper paste

Varnish sealer (optional)

Wallpaper brush

Sponge

Pail of water

Foam roller and tray
(optional)

What You Do

1. Tear the paper into 10- to
12-inch (26.7 to 30.5 cm)
shapes, and crinkle the
shapes.

2. Starting at one of the
room's top corners, brush
paste on a 2-foot (61 cm)
area of a wall.

3. Use a shape that has a
straight edge, place it at
the ceiling line, and paste it
gently to the wall with the
brush. Be sure not to brush
the raised wrinkles out of
the bag's surface. Carefully
smooth out the excess
paste with the sponge.

4. Apply another piece
next to the first, overlapping the edges about 1/4
inch (6 mm).

5. Continue working in this
way, using pieces with
straight edges at the ceiling
line. You'll also want to use
pieces with straight edges
at corners and along baseboards. All your other
pieces should have torn
edges all the way around.

6. To make the treatment
more durable, roll on a varnish sealer after 24 hours.

VARIATION

If you want a
more formal,
velvety look,
brush the
paper flat to
the wall, leav-
ing only a hint
of crinkle.

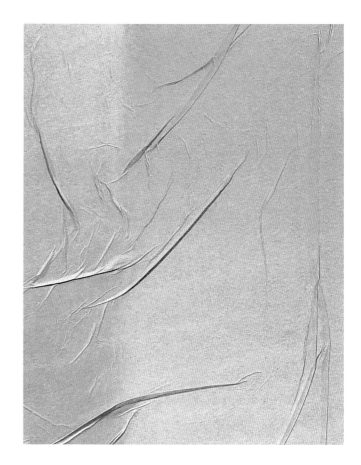

playing card chair rail

Designer: Lyna Farkas

WITH THIS DO-IT-YOURSELF BORDER, THE ARTISTRY IS IN THE
APPLICATION. TWIST, TURN, AND FLIP YOUR CARDS UNTIL YOU'RE
HAPPY WITH THE HAND YOU'VE DEALT.

What You Need

Satin latex paint
(optional)

Playing cards in two dif-
ferent colors or styles
(For the best adhesion,
you need cards that
aren't plastic coated.
Check flea markets and
antique stores.)

Heavy-weight
wallpaper paste

Clear varnish or amber
shellac

Roller tray and roller with
¼-inch (6 mm) nap
(optional)

Tape measure

Level

Paste brush

Seam roller

Sponge

Pail of water

Sponge roller

What You Do

1. Measure to chair-rail
height (approximately 33 to
36 inches [83.8 to 91 cm]),
and use the level to mark
the line across each wall.

2. If you want to paint your
wall two different colors to
coordinate with your cards,
as we have, do so now. Use
the line as a guide. Let the
paint dry.

3. Paste the bottom side of
first card and press it in
place on the line at one end
of the wall.

4. Paste the next card next
to the first, overlapping it in
some way.

5. Continue to apply cards
horizontally down the
length of the wall, turning
the cards at different angles
as you press them into
place. Use the seam roller to
press the cards down as you
go and the dampened
sponge to clean off any
excess paste.

6. As you approach the
other end of the wall, space
the cards carefully, so you
don't end up with a gap at
the end. Let the cards dry
overnight.

7. With the sponge roller,
roll on a protective coat of
clear varnish or, if you want
an aged look, amber shellac.

Variations

Postcards, soup-can labels, and thin
cardboard coasters featuring logos
are other options for chair rails to
suit specific styles.

sheet music

Designer: Lyna Farkas

MAYBE YOU HAVE A FAMILY ROOM YOU PLAN TO DECORATE WITH
SHOW POSTERS AND A PIANO. OR PERHAPS YOU JUST HAVE A QUIET
CORNER YOU'D LIKE TO LIVEN UP. EITHER WAY, SHEETS FROM MUSICAL
SCORES WILL MAKE YOUR WALLS SING.

What You Need

Wallpaper paste

Supply of sheet music

Latex varnish

Plumb line

Paste brush

Sponge

Pail of water

Trim guide

Utility knife

Foam roller and tray

What You Do

1. Hang a plumb line in a corner of the wall, and mark the line in pencil, so you have a gauge for hanging the sheets straight.

2. Start working at the top corner of the wall. Brush paste on a 2-foot by 2-foot (61 x 61 cm) section of the wall.

3. Place a sheet of music on the paste, aligning its edge with the plumb line, and smooth it out with a damp sponge, removing excess paste.

4. Place the next sheet directly below the first sheet, overlapping about ¼ inch (6 mm), to allow for shrinkage.

5. Repeat, working down the wall. If the last piece needs trimming at the baseboard, use the trim guide and utility knife.

6. Move back to the top, and apply a second vertical row of sheets next to the first row. Continue working in this way until you reach the opposite corner of the wall.

7. If you're papering more than one wall, let the sheet music wrap around the corner, if that's how it falls. Use the trim guide to make sure it fits snugly into the corner. If you're papering just one wall, use the trim guide and utility knife to cut the excess paper at the corner, if necessary.

8. Finish papering the room's other walls, if you plan to do so, and let the walls dry overnight.

9. The next day, use the foam roller to apply a clear coat of latex varnish over the sheet music.

VARIATIONS

Try papering a kitchen nook with old handwritten recipes, a wall in a child's room with sheets of bright wrapping paper or pages from a story-book, or a wall in a home office with spreadsheets, graphs, and pie charts.

chapter 5
wallpaper accents

What You Need

Metal containers

Raised-pattern, paintable wallpaper

Wallpaper paste

Acrylic paints in black and silver

Scissors

Pasting brush

Utility knife

Stippling brush

Rinse water and cup

bins & planters

Designer: Diana Light

FROM PLANTERS AND UTENSIL HOLDERS TO STORAGE BOXES AND FILE BINS, CONTAINERS ARE A FACT OF ANY LIFE THAT ASPIRES TO BE ORGANIZED. WALLPAPER OFFERS AN EASY WAY TO HELP THOSE CONTAINERS LOOK STYLISH AS THEY CREATE ORDER.

What You Do

1. Roll out a section of wallpaper, pattern side down, and trace around each side of the container you plan to cover. If your container has a lip, take it into account when you mark the pieces. It's better to make your pieces slightly larger than you need rather than risk making them too small. You can trim away any excess paper later.

2. Cut out the pieces.

3. Paste the pieces one at a time, and apply them to the container, neatly aligning the sides of the paper with the sides of the container.

4. Let the paper dry, then carefully trim away any excess with the utility knife.

5. Use the stippling brush to cover all of the wallpaper sections with one of your paint colors. Be sure you get paint into all the recessed areas. Let the paint dry.

6. Clean the brush, then use it to apply the second paint color lightly over the wallpaper's raised sections. Let the paint dry.

What You Need

Raised-pattern, paintable wallpaper

Picture frame

Acrylic or latex paint

Tape

Ruler

Scissors

Paintbrush

Craft knife

What You Do

1. Measure and mark a section of wallpaper to fit inside the frame, then cut it out.

2. Paint the wallpaper and let it dry.

3. Using the wallpaper pattern as a guide, cut sections out of the mat with the craft knife to create display openings.

4. Tape the edges of your photos or pieces of artwork to the back of the mat, and fit the mat into the frame.

textured picture mat

Designer: Heather Smith

PICK A RAISED-PATTERN, PAINTABLE PAPER WITH A DESIGN LIKE THIS ONE—WITH SHAPES THAT MAKE FOR EASY CUTOUTS—AND YOU CAN CUSTOMIZE THE COLOR AND STYLE OF A PICTURE MAT.

What You Need

Architectural columns

Paint stripper

Spackle

Sandpaper

Primer

Semigloss paint in white or another color of your choice

Wallpaper that looks like marble

Wallpaper paste

Small trowel for applying spackle

Several paintbrushes

Flexible cloth tape measure

Pasting brush

What You Do

1. If your columns need some cleaning up, strip off the old paint, fill any cracks and holes with spackle, lightly sand them, then apply a coat of primer.

2. Once the primer is dry, apply a coat of paint.

3. Determine which portion of each column you want to paper. Use the cloth tape measure to calculate the size of the wallpaper strip you need for each.

4. Cut your pieces of wallpaper, and wrap them into place temporarily, to make sure the fit is right. Adjust the sizes of the strips, if necessary.

5. Once you're satisfied with the fit of the wallpaper strips, apply paste to them one at a time, and apply them. Position the paper so the seams are on what will become the backs of your columns. Smooth any wrinkles out with your hand.

faux marble columns

Designer: Megan Kirby

YOU CAN FIND COLUMNS LIKE THESE AT ARCHITECTURAL SALVAGE STORES. THEY'RE GENERALLY SOMEWHAT WEATHERED AND WILL NEED SOME PREPARATION BEFORE YOU PAPER, BUT THE PROCESS OF WRAPPING WALLPAPER AROUND THE BASE IS STILL LOADS EASIER THAN PAINTING ON A FAUX FINISH.

mousepads

Designer: Heather Smith

TODAY, YOU CAN FIND WALLPAPER BORDERS IN WONDERFULLY OUTRAGEOUS
DESIGNS, FEATURING EVERYTHING FROM CHORUS LINES TO ICE CREAM CONES.
PICK A FEW—OR USE SCRAPS OF FAVORITE FULL-SIZE PAPERS—TO CUSTOMIZE
MOUSEPADS FOR GIFTS, PARTY FAVORS, OR YOUR OWN DESK.

Wallpaper (Before you start, make sure the pattern you've selected doesn't confuse your computer mouse.)

Black foam

Newspaper

Super-strength spray adhesive

Scissors

Black felt-tip pen

Craft knife

What You Do

1. Cut out the section of wallpaper you want to feature on your mousepad.

2. Set the image on the foam pad and trace around it.

3. Cut the shape from the rest of the foam, and set it on an open sheet of newspaper.

4. Spray the back of the wallpaper image and the top of the foam shape with adhesive. Align the image over the foam, and press the two together along one edge. Smooth out any wrinkles as you press the surfaces together.

5. Use the black pen around the edges of the mousepad to make a dark, consistent border where the wallpaper and foam meet.

jazzed-up writing table

Designer: Derick Tickle

TAKING HIS CUE FROM A SPIRITED PIECE OF WALLPAPER, THIS DESIGNER CUT AND PASTED A PIANO KEYBOARD ALONG THE BOTTOM EDGE OF HIS TABLE. BUT HE COULD JUST AS EASILY HAVE USED A DIFFERENT PAPER TO INSPIRE TYPEWRITER KEYS, AWNING STRIPES, A ROW OF FLOWER POTS—OR NO BOTTOM BORDER AT ALL. THINK OF A TABLETOP AS THE EASIEST OF SURFACES TO WALLPAPER (IT'S NOTHING MORE THAN A SMALL, FLAT PANEL); THEN SEE WHERE YOUR PAPER LEADS YOU.

What You Need

Writing table

Sandpaper

Sanding sealer or shellac

Wallpaper primer

Wallpaper (For this design, choose a wallpaper with a musical motif. You also need small scraps of white paper and black paper.)

Wood stains in a variety of colors that coordinate with your wallpaper

White craft glue

Non-yellowing satin varnish

Tack cloth

Ruler

Paintbrushes

Pasting brush

Smoother

Damp sponge

Metal straightedge

Utility knife

Extra-fine felt-tip pen

What You Do

1. Lightly sand the table to remove any rough edges or splinters, then use a tack cloth to remove the dust.

2. Mark out a 2-inch (10.2 cm) border around the sides and back edge of the tabletop. You'll stain the border in step 6 and paper the panel within it beginning in step 9.

3. To ensure even color and prevent blotchiness, apply one coat of sanding sealer or clear shellac to all parts of the table except the panel inside the border, where you'll apply wallpaper. Let it dry for two hours.

4. Apply one coat of wallpaper primer to the panel on the tabletop, and let it dry.

5. Use a fine sandpaper to sand all the surfaces you sealed, making sure to sand only in the direction of the natural wood grain.

6. Apply colored wood stains to all areas of the table but the top central panel. Make different elements of the table (the legs, drawer, knob, and the border you marked in step 2) different colors. When the stains dry, apply a second coat, if necessary. The stain should allow the natural wood grain to show through.

7. For a keyboard design like this one, mark a pencil line that runs 4 inches (10.2 cm) in from the front edge of the tabletop and between the two side borders. This line now becomes the bottom of your tabletop's center panel.

8. Cut a piece of wallpaper 2 inches (5.1 cm) larger all the way around than the table's center panel.

9. Paste the paper and apply it, smoothing out any air pockets with a smoother or a damp sponge.

10. With the metal straightedge and utility knife, carefully trim the panel to size. Make sure that the edges are firmly pressed down and no air bubbles remain. Remove any excess paste from the surrounding areas, and let everything dry overnight.

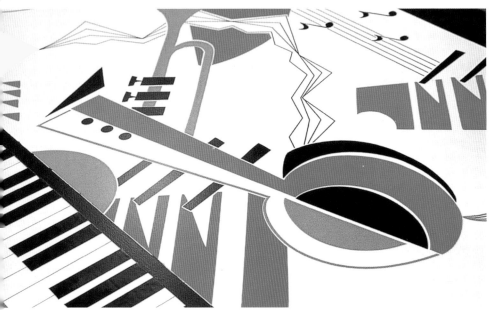

them out individually with the metal straightedge and utility knife.

13. Glue in all the white keys along the 4-inch (10.2) space at the front edge of the table. The white craft glue will help keep the edges from curling.

14. Glue the black keys directly over the white keys.

15. When all keys are in place, remove any adhesive residue with a damp sponge, and let them dry overnight.

16. Create a "shadow" between the keys, using a pencil or an extra-fine felt-tip pen.

17. Give the entire piece two coats of varnish to provide a durable and washable surface.

11. To give a realistic feel to the keyboard, you'll want to cut and glue each key individually. Make cardboard templates first. The white keys should be 4 inches (10.2 cm) by $3/4$ inch (1.9 cm). The black keys should be 2 $1/2$ inches (6.4 cm) by $1/2$ inch (1.3 cm).

12. Use the templates to draw keys on the white and black papers. Cut

papering small
spaces & secret places

Designer: Lyna Farkas

THINK OF ALL THE SMALL, FLAT SURFACES YOU COULD TRANSFORM FROM ORDINARY TO DELIGHTFUL WITH A SWATCH OF SPECIAL WALLPAPER. THE BACKS OF OPEN SHELVES AND GLASS-FRONT CABINETS COUNT. SO DOES THE STRIP OF WALL OVER YOUR MANTEL. AND DON'T FORGET THE HIDDEN SPOTS WHERE SOME PRETTY PAPER CAN BE YOUR LITTLE SECRET, FROM THE INSIDES OF CUPBOARD DOORS TO THE BOTTOMS OF SOCK DRAWERS. BONUS: THIS IS A GREAT WAY TO INCORPORATE A DARING OR EXPENSIVE PAPER THAT YOU MIGHT NOT USE TO COVER AN ENTIRE ROOM.

What You Need

Primer

Wallpaper

Wallpaper paste

Paint tray and sponge roller

Tape measure

Scissors

Pasting brush

Water pail

Sponge

Trim guide

Utility knife

What You Do

1. Start with a clean, flat surface. If you're papering behind shelves or some other fixture, it's best if you can remove them before you start; then reinstall them when you're finished.

2. Prime the surface.

3. Measure the space you want to paper, and cut your wallpaper strips, adding 4 inches (10.2 cm) to the length of each. If you have a pattern you need to match from strip to strip, cut the strips accordingly.

4. Paste the wallpaper and apply it, butting your strips together and matching the pattern across the join, if necessary. You should have 2 inches (5.1 cm) of excess paper at the top and bottom of each strip, where it meets the edge of the panel or the panel molding.

5. Trim the excess paper using a trim guide and utility knife.

Tip: If you're papering cupboards, kitchen shelves, or other heavy-use areas, be sure to keep the papered areas clean. It's difficult to remove stains from wallpaper once they've set.

victorian print-room screen

Designer: Lyna Farkas

THE CENTRAL PANEL OF THIS ELEGANT WALLPAPERED SCREEN
IS A TRIBUTE TO THE WHIMSICAL, 18TH-CENTURY PRACTICE OF
CUTTING OUT PRINTS AND PASTING THEM ON THE WALLS.

What You Need

Solid-wood standing
screen (Or, fashion your
own screen by hinging
together three panels of
3/4-inch [1.9 cm] smooth
plywood.)

Fine- and medium-grit
sandpaper

Tack cloth

Latex primer

Gold latex paint (enough
to paint the backs of the
panels)

Wallpaper liner (enough
to cover the three panels)

Wallpapers of your
choice: one to serve as
the background for the
two flanking panels,
another to overlay on the
flanking panels, gold
paper for framing the
flanking panels, paper
with a border to use for
edging the flanking pan-
els, patterned paper for
the upper section of the
central panel, and
embossed paper for the
bottom half of the central
panel

Black-and-white copy-
right-free photocopied
images (Choose
Victorian-style images
that complement your
wallpapers, along with
images such as ropes
and swags you can use
to link them. You can also
find such images on spe-
cialty wallpaper borders.)

Wallpaper paste

Artist's acrylic paint
in raw umber

Artist's low-tack
masking tape

Drop cloth

2 paint rollers with a 1/4-
inch (6 mm) nap

Paint trays with dispos-
able liners

Sharp paper scissors

Ruler

Pasting brush

Smoothing brush

Sponge

Level

Craft knife

Piece of glass to use as
a cutting surface or a cutting mat

Small paper scissors

Plastic container for mixing paint

3-inch (7.6 cm) paintbrush

What You Do

1. Lightly sand the front and
back of each panel of your
screen, then wipe down the
panels with the tack cloth.

2. Spread out the drop cloth
on your work surface or
floor, and use the nap roller
to apply primer to the sides
and backs of the screen's
panels. Allow it to dry, then
apply primer to the fronts of
the panels.

3. With a clean nap roller, roll
two coats of gold paint on
the sides and backs of the
panels, allowing the paint to
dry between coats. Flip the
panels over after they're dry.

4. Use scissors and the ruler
to cut out three identical
pieces of wallpaper liner to
fit the front (unpainted side)
of each panel. Set one of the
pieces aside for later.

5. Brush paste onto the back
of one of the pieces of lining
paper, book the paper, and
let the paste set for a couple
of minutes.

6. Unfold the upper half of
the paper, hold the edge
between your thumb and fingers, and position it along
the top of one of the flanking
panels. Slide the wallpaper
into position.

7. Use the smoothing brush
to press the paper against
the panel, brushing down the
center firmly toward the
edges. Unfold the lower half
of the paper, and brush it
against the panel.

8. Remove any air bubbles
under the paper by carefully
lifting the nearest corner of
the paper and rebrushing it
against the panel. Dampen

the sponge, and use it to wipe away excess paste from around the edges of the paper.

9. Repeat the process to place liner paper on the other flanking panel.

10. Once the liner is in place, cut two identical pieces of the background wallpaper to fit the front of each flanking panel. Paste the wallpaper to the panels, following the same procedure you used for the liner.

11. From another wallpaper, cut two identical rectangular pieces to fit down the middle of the two flanking panels. If your panels feature triangular crests at the top, cut pieces to fit all three of them from the same paper. Set aside one of the triangular pieces for later.

12. On each flanking panel, find the center, then use the level and ruler to lightly draw two horizontal lines to mark the position of the rectangular piece you cut in step 10.

Paste and apply the pieces to the flanking panels.

13. Paste and apply the triangular pieces to the crests of the flanking panels.

14. Cut and apply a 1-inch (2.5 cm) frame-like border around each of the rectangular pieces. To do so, make each strip about 6 inches (15.2 cm) longer than necessary. Paste the backs of the strips, leaving about 3 inches (7.6 cm) unpasted on each end. Smooth the strips into place around the rectangular panels, overlapping the ends. Where the strips overlap at each corner, use the ruler to lightly draw a diagonal, then use the utility knife to carefully cut the strips along the lines. Butt the ends of the border strips together as you smooth them firmly into place with a damp sponge. Wipe away any excess paste.

15. Measure and cut border strips to fit around the outer edges of the two flanking panels, using the same process.

16. Paste the third piece of liner in place on the front of the central panel.

17. Cut out a piece of the patterned wallpaper to fit the upper two-thirds of the panel (not including the crest, if your panel has one). Paste the paper in place.

18. Paste and position the triangular piece you cut out for the central panel's crest (if your panel has one), so it butts against the patterned wallpaper.

19. Cut a 1-inch (2.5 cm) strip from the gold wallpaper that fits over the seam where the top and middle papers meet. Paste it into place over the seam.

20. Cut a piece from the embossed wallpaper to fit the bottom section of the panel, plus about one inch (2.5 cm). Paste the paper to the panel so the top edge overlaps the bottom edge of the middle paper.

21. With the nap roller, apply a coat of gold latex paint to the embossed wall-

paper. When the paint is dry, apply a second coat.

22. Lay your black-and-white images on your cutting surface, and trim them with the craft knife or with small paper scissors.

23. Make a wash for the cutout pieces to give them a sepia tone by mixing two parts of acrylic raw umber paint with one part water in the plastic container. Use the paintbrush to apply the wash. Let it dry.

24. Position the images on the central panel. Move them around until you achieve the look you want, using low-tack masking tape to hold them in place. Step back and make sure they're level and spaced as you wish.

25. Starting with the outermost pieces, remove them one at a time, apply a thin coat of paste to the back, and reposition them. Press the pieces around the edges with a damp sponge, removing the excess paste.

lampshade

Designer: Diana Light

WHAT COULD BE EASIER THAN WRAPPING A PIECE OF MARVELOUS WALLPAPER AROUND A TUBE OF POSTER BOARD? IF YOU WANT TO GIVE NEW LIFE TO AN OLD LAMP, THERE'S NOT MUCH MORE TO IT THAN THAT.

What You Need

Lampshade with hardware to fit your lamp base

White poster board

Wallpaper

Flexible cloth tape measure

Scissors

High-temperature hot glue gun and glue stick

Spray adhesive

What You Do

1. Decide how tall you want your lampshade, then measure the circumference of the lamp's hardware and add 1 inch (2.5 cm).

2. Use the measurements to mark pieces of poster board and wallpaper. Cut them out.

3. Cut the shade material away from the hardware end of the existing lampshade, and discard the material.

4. Wrap the poster-board piece into a cylinder around the remaining hardware frame. Use the glue gun to attach the poster board to the frame and to glue the seam of the poster board.

5. Spray the back of the wallpaper piece with adhesive, and attach it around the poster-board cylinder.

SAFETY TIP:
Use bulbs no stronger than 60 watts in your new lamp.

wallpaper wall art

Designer: Lyna Farkas

IF YOU'VE RUN OUT OF PLACES TO PAPER BUT HAVE SOME FABULOUS
SCRAPS YOU'RE DYING TO PUT TO USE, CUT THEM INTO SQUARES,
MOUNT THEM OR FRAME THEM, AND THINK OF THEM AS INSTANT ART.

What You Need

Wallpapers in various colors and textures, cut into 12 16-inch (40.6 cm) squares

Wallpaper border paste

12 pieces of heavy cardboard or poster board, each 16 inches (40.6 cm) square

Pasting brush

Smoother

Sponge

Pail of water

12 stick-mounting picture hangers

What You Do

1. Paste the back of one of the wallpaper squares, place it on one of the cardboard pieces, and smooth it.

2. Remove any excess paste with the damp sponge.

3. Attach the rest of the wallpaper squares to the cardboard squares in the same way; then let the pieces dry overnight.

4. Affix a picture hanger to the top back center of each papered square, and hang the squares on the wall in a grid of three rows of four squares, as shown here, or in any configuration you like.

variation

What You Need

5 different pieces of wallpaper, each approximately 13 ½ x 13 ½ inches (34.3 x 34.3 cm)

Piece of corrugated cardboard, approximately 29 x 29 inches (73.7 x 73.7 cm)

4 pieces of foam-core board, each 1 x 1 inch (2.5 x 2.5 cm)

Piece of thin cardboard, 13 ½ x 13 ½ inches (34.3 x 34.3 cm)

Wallpaper paste

White craft glue

Pasting brush

Sponge

Pail of water

Ruler

Utility knife

What You Do

1. Decide how you want to arrange your five pieces of wallpaper. Four will serve as the background, and one will overlap the others at the center. Set the center piece aside.

2. Make a 1-inch (2.5 cm) border around the edge of the large piece of corrugated cardboard.

3. Brush paste on the back of the square of wallpaper you want at the top left of your design and apply it, aligning it with the border line you drew in step 2.

4. Smooth the piece down with a damp sponge, and remove any excess paste.

5. Apply the top right piece, butting the edges of the two top squares together, then apply the two pieces below. If the paper edges don't join tightly, overlap them by ¼ inch (6 mm), and use the ruler and utility knife to cut down the center of the join. Remove the excess pieces of both edges.

6. Mark spots 6 inches (15.2 cm) from the design's center, horizontally and vertically on each side. Glue the foam-core squares at these points.

7. Paste the fifth wallpaper piece and apply it to the thin 13 ½ x 13 ½-inch (34.3 x 34.3 cm) piece of cardboard.

8. Glue the final square on top of the foam-core pieces, centering it.

9. Mat and frame your piece.

stove hood

Designer: Lyna Farkas

NOTHING BEATS A FINISHING TOUCH. ONCE YOU'RE FINALLY SATISFIED WITH THE WALLS, CABINETS, COUNTER TOPS, AND THE REST, WHY NOT COMPLETE YOUR KITCHEN BY COVERING THE STOVE HOOD WITH A COMPLEMENTARY WALLPAPER? HERE, WE USED ONE THAT'S A SMALLER-SCALE VERSION OF THE PAPER ON THE WALLS. USE THIS SAME TECHNIQUE TO PAPER OVER ANY METAL SURFACE.

What You Need

Cleaning mixture of ammonia and water

Oil-based, rust-proof paint

Acrylic primer

Wallpaper

Wallpaper paste

Several small paintbrushes

Utility knife

Measuring tool

Sponge

Pail of water

Trim guide

What You Do

1. Clean any dirt and grease build-up off the metal hood with the ammonia-water mixture.

2. Apply rust-proof paint to the hood, and let it dry for 24 hours.

3. Apply acrylic primer and let it dry for 24 hours.

4. Cut the lengths of wallpaper you need to cover the front and both sides of your hood, allowing a 2-inch (5.1 cm) overlap on each end and a ½-inch (1.3 cm) overlap on top.

5. Paste and apply the front strip so it's flush with the bottom edge of the hood. Press the extra ½ inch (1.3 cm) over onto the top of the hood. Cut the two ends to a ½-inch (1.3 cm) overlap, and press the overlaps around the corners.

6. Paste and apply the side pieces. Trim the front edges so they cover the ½-inch (1.3 cm) overlaps from the front strip. Trim the other edges at the wall. Press the extra ½ inch (1.3 cm) over onto the top of the hood.

7. Cut a piece of wallpaper to fit the size and shape of your hood. Paste and apply it, neatly covering all the overlaps.

quick-change cabinet doors

Designer: Terry Taylor

THE THING ABOUT GLASS-FRONT CABINET DOORS, OF COURSE, IS
THAT THEY REVEAL WHATEVER DISARRAY MAY BE LURKING
BEHIND. REPLACE THE GLASS PANES WITH WALLPAPER INSERTS
FOR A FAST MASK—OR JUST AN EASY CHANGE OF DECOR.

What You Need

Small plastic bag

Foam-core board

Newspaper

Spray adhesive

Wallpaper

Ruler

Utility knife

Scissors

Smoother

Note: Foam-core
board is a great
temporary surface for
these wallpaper
inserts. If you want
your change to your
cabinets to be more
permanent, use a thin
luan board instead,
and substitute wallpa-
per paste for the
aerosol glue.

What You Do

1. Remove the glass panes
from your cabinet
doors, and place any hardware you remove in the
plastic bag.

2. Measure the glass
panes, then measure and
mark the size of each different pane on the foam-
core board. Cut out the
foam-core pieces with the
utility knife.

3. Measure and mark
identical pieces on the
back side of the wallpaper,
and cut out the wallpaper
pieces.

4. Cover your work area
with lots and lots of newspaper to protect the sur-
face from glue overspray.
It's a good idea to spread
the newspapers out over
a larger area than you
think you need to cover.

5. Carefully spray the
foam-core pieces with an
even coat of adhesive.

6. One piece at a time, lay
the wallpaper on the
foam-core board, and
smooth out any wrinkles
or air bubbles. Let the
glue dry.

7. Place the boards in the
door panels. Secure the
boards with the hardware
you removed in step 1.

VINTAGE PRINTS

Some of the most popular new wallpapers are actually reproductions of classic patterns from decades ago. Shown here in full-room settings, many of these pretty, delicate papers are perfect choices for small projects, such as the one on the preceding page, that add accents in the kitchen.

antiquing new paper

SOMETIMES, AGED AND ABRADED WALLPAPER IS JUST WHAT YOU WANT IF THE REST OF YOUR SETTING FEATURES ACCENTS SUCH AS WEATHERED WOOD AND FLEA MARKET FINDS. HERE'S HOW TO GIVE BRAND NEW PAPER THE CHARMING LOOK OF HAVING BEEN AROUND A WHILE.

What You Need

Medium-grit sandpaper block

Tube of raw or burnt umber acrylic paint

Sponge

Pail of water

Plastic bowl

4-inch (10.2 cm) brush

Cheesecloth

What You Do

1. Starting at the top of the wallpapered area, sand in various directions, lightly at first. Use more pressure until you achieve the amount of distress you're after. You want bits of the papered surface showing through here and there. Go easy along the seams, which are more delicate.

2. Wipe down the sanded area with a damp sponge. Let it dry.

3. Squeeze a small amount of burnt umber paint into the bowl. Water it down a bit, but don't let it get too watery.

4. Starting again at the top of the wallpapered area, brush the paint onto a 3-foot by 3-foot (91.4 x 91.4 cm) section.

5. Bunch up the cheesecloth, and pat it over the paint to soften it.

6. Continue working in small sections as you paint and soften the entire area.

TIP: As you work the watered-down paint onto the wallpaper, you may notice some darker areas where you've overlapped the paint. To avoid a regular pattern of overlaps, brush the paint on in puzzle-piece shapes. This will break up the overlaps and fool the eye.

copper-look frame

Designer: Heather Smith

PAINTABLE WALLPAPER COMES IN DESIGNS RESEMBLING
EVERYTHING FROM PLASTER MOLDING TO METAL CEILING TILES.
TREAT YOURS WITH A PAINT THAT SUITS THE STYLE, AND YOU
CAN CREATE ALL SORTS OF HANDSOME PICTURE FRAMES.

What You Need

Frame that's at least 2
inches (5.1 cm) wide

Scrap piece of textured
wallpaper

Super-strength spray
adhesive

Copper metallic paint

Clear gloss
polyurethane finish

Ruler

Craft knife

Cutting mat or maga-
zines to protect your
work surface

Small paintbrush

What You Do

1. Remove the glass and backing from
the frame. Set the frame facedown on
the back of the piece of wallpaper. Trace
the inside and outside edges of the
frame onto the wallpaper.

2. Measure the depth and the width of
the frame. Add the two measurements
together, and use the total to make
guide marks on the paper around the
outside edge you traced in step 1. Use
the guide marks to draw new outside
edges. The excess will give you enough
paper to wrap around the sides and
back of the frame.

3. Cut out the traced piece, using the
ruler as a guide for your craft knife.

4. Spray adhesive on the back of the
wallpaper piece and on the front of the
frame, then press the frame in place on
the wallpaper. Smooth the wallpaper
against the frame.

5. Cut the wallpaper to fit the corners of
the frame. First, draw lines at each corner that extend from the edges of the
frame to the edges of the paper, making
boxes at each corner (see figure 1). Cut
out the boxes, and fold the remaining
paper over the edges of the frame to
check the fit. Trim away any overlapping
paper, so the remaining paper fits
smoothly on the back of the frame.

6. Spray the sides and back of the
frame, then fold the paper around the
frame, smoothing it in place.

7. Paint the front of the frame with
metallic copper paint. Once it's dry,
paint the sides and back of the frame,
and let them dry.

8. Protect the paint by spraying a coat
of clear gloss finish over the frame.

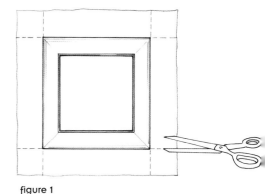

figure 1

storage boxes

Designer: Heather Smith

CARDBOARD CONTAINERS SHAPED LIKE HATBOXES ARE AVAILABLE AT ANY CRAFT STORE. COVER A SET IN A COMBINATION OF TOILE PAPERS, AND YOU HAVE SOME HANDY STORAGE BOXES MASQUERADING AS ROMANTIC DISPLAY PIECES.

What You Need

Acrylic gloss paints in colors that coordinate with your wallpapers

Assorted cardboard containers with lids

Toile wallpapers in assorted colors and patterns

Super-strength spray adhesive

Glass cleaner

Paintbrush

Scissors

Flexible cloth tape measure

Ruler

Rag

What You Do

1. Paint the bottom and lid of each container with a paint color that complements one of your wallpapers. Let them dry.

2. Measure the height and circumference of your first container.

3. Cut a piece of wallpaper from one of your rolls. Make it larger than you need to cover your first container, but manageable enough to work with. Locate a section of the paper that has a pattern you like, mark out the dimensions of your first container, and cut out the piece.

4. If the container's circumference is greater than the width of the wallpaper, you'll need to cut a smaller piece of wallpaper to fill the gap. Make the patching piece 1 inch (2.5 cm) wider than the gap, and mark and cut it from a section where the pattern matches the first piece as much as possible.

5. Set the container on its side on the back side of the wallpaper. Spray adhesive on the sides of the container and on the back side of the paper. Give the adhesive 30 seconds to become tacky, then carefully wrap the paper around the container, smoothing out any wrinkles as you work.

6. Spray adhesive on the back of the patch piece, if you need one, and press it in place, matching the pattern with the larger piece as closely as possible.

7. Set the covered container aside and wipe down your work surface with the rag and glass cleaner to remove any adhesive residue before covering another container.

Topping It Off: To cover a lid, measure and cut a strip of wallpaper to fit around the rim, then trace the shape of the top onto the back of a piece of wallpaper, and cut it out. Glue both pieces in place with spray adhesive.

tables & nightstands

THE PLAIN, FLAT SURFACES OF END TABLES, NIGHTSTANDS, AND OTHER SMALL PIECES OF FURNITURE ARE THE PERFECT PLACES FOR SWATCHES OF LEFTOVER PAPER. COVER THE FRONTS OF THEIR DRAWERS AND DOORS AND THE TOPS OF THEIR SHELVES TO TIE THEM NEATLY INTO THEIR SURROUNDINGS.

french country telephone table

Designer: Diana Light

What You Need

Small table with lower shelf and drawer

Wallpaper in a simple pattern, such as gingham

Wallpaper with a simple motif, such as cherries (Try to make sure the background color of both papers is the same.)

Drawer pull that coordinates with one of your papers

Straightedge

Scissors and/or a craft knife

Wallpaper paste

Pasting brush

Smoother

What You Do

1. If you can disassemble your table, do so. Roll out a strip of your patterned paper, pattern-side up, place the table's bottom shelf on top of the paper, and lightly trace around it, making sure the paper's pattern lines are aligned with the shelf's edge. If you're unable to disassemble your table, use the straightedge to carefully push the patterned paper to the edges of the shelf, and mark the edges. Cut out the traced or marked piece.

2. Brush paste on the back of the piece and paste it to the top of the shelf. Smooth out any bubbles with the smoother.

3. Use the scissors or craft knife to cut out pieces of the motif from your second paper.

4. Paste the pieces to the front of your table's door, and attach the coordinating drawer pull.

coordinating nightstand

Designer: Lyna Farkas

What You Need

Nightstand with flat front panel

Remnant of your bedroom wallpaper

Wallpaper paste

Tape measure

Scissors

Pasting brush

Trim guide

Utility knife

Smoother

Damp sponge

What You Do

1. Measure the panel you want to paper and cut a piece of wallpaper that's 4 inches (10.2 cm) wider and longer.

2. Paste the wallpaper and apply it. You should have 2 inches (5.1 cm) of excess paper at the top and bottom and on each edge.

3. Trim the excess paper using the trim guide and utility knife.

4. Smooth out any bubbles in the paper with the smoother, and remove any excess paste with the sponge.

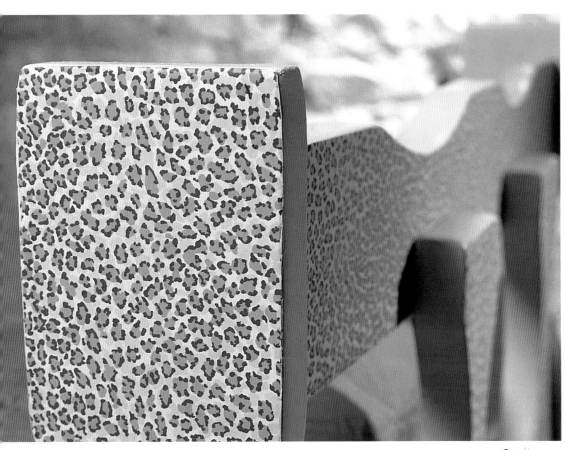

pink leopard bed

Designer: Diana Light

WHEN YOUR LITTLE ONE IS SET ON A SPECIFIC LOOK—BE IT WIZARDS, LADYBUGS, OR LEOPARD PRINT—WALLPAPER IS AN EASY WAY TO HELP A BED OR ANY FURNITURE PIECE JOIN THE THEME.

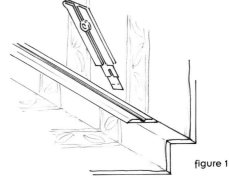

figure 1

What You Need

Wooden headboard and footboard with flat surfaces

Sandpaper

Wallpaper

Wallpaper paste

Semigloss paint in a coordinating color

Scissors

Straightedge

Pasting brush

Utility knife with new blades

Smoother

Sponge

Pail of water

Flat paintbrush

What You Do

1. Disassemble your bed to make the headboard and footboard easier to work with.

2. Decide which areas you want to cover, and lightly sand them if they're glossy, then clean and dry them.

3. Roll out a strip of wall-paper, pattern-side down, lay one of the pieces on it, trace around the piece, and cut it out. If you need to fit the paper around raised sections, don't trace them. Instead, use the straightedge to push the paper up to the sec-tion's edge and to hold the paper in place, then use the utility knife to cut along the straightedge (see figure 1). If you need to use more than one strip of wallpaper to cover a section, follow the steps in Wallpapering Basics for matching the paper's pat-tern across the join.

4. Brush paste on the cut-out wallpaper and apply it to the bed piece. Smooth out any bubbles with the smoother, and use the damp sponge to remove any excess paste. Let the paste dry.

5. Repeat steps 3 and 4 to cover your other bed piece, then paint the accent areas.

**Ellipse
Pattern for
Wallpaper
Shapes,
page 54**

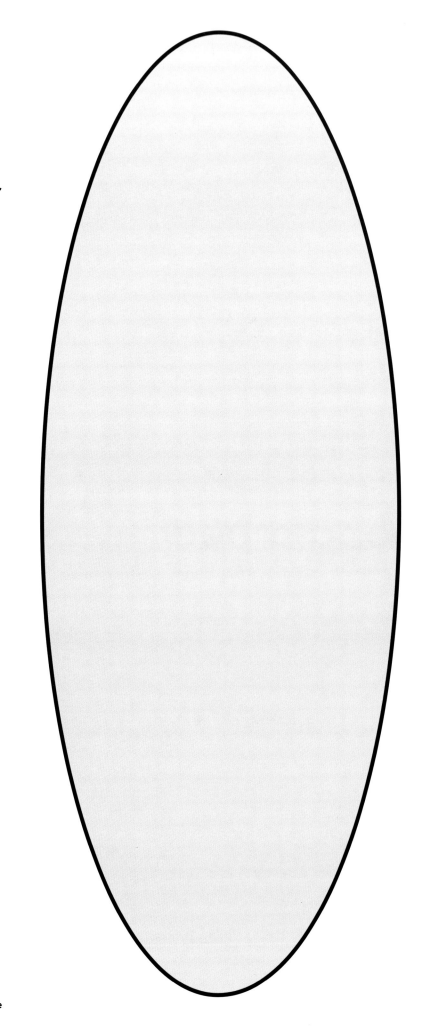

acknowledgments

Abundant thanks to:

• Derick Tickle and Asheville-Buncombe Technical Community College, Jamesa B. Selleck, and Sara-Beth Black for welcoming our cameras and crew into their beautifully wallpapered spaces.

• Holladay Paint and Wallpaper, Asheville, North Carolina, for keeping dozens and dozens of wallpaper orders straight.

• Allen Funk's Wallpapers and Kathryn Long of Ambiance Interiors, both of Asheville, North Carolina, for advice and insight.

• Enviro-Depot, downtown Asheville, North Carolina, for lending us a huge supply of colorful, creative props.

And finally, much thanks to the generous companies that allowed us to reprint their photographs:

Gramercy Wallcoverings, a brand of F. Schumacher & Co.: pages 23 (upper left and lower right); 26 (center); 30 (lower); 57; 114 (lower). Courtesy of: Gramercy Wallcoverings, 79 Madison Avenue, New York, NY 10016. Phone: 212-213-7900, Fax: 212-213-7640, Consumers: 800-988-7775, Retailers: 800-523-1200, www.fschumacher.com

Imperial Home Decor Group (IHDG): pages 10-11; 13 (upper right); 35. Courtesy of: Imperial Home Decor Group, 23645 Mercantile Road, Cleveland, OH 44122, Phone: 1-888-608-5943, Fax: 1-800-444-7865, www.ihdg.com

Seabrook Wallcoverings, Inc: pages 8 (far left, second from left, and upper right); 9 (upper right); 13 (lower left); 15 (upper); 17 (upper left); 18 (all) ; 19 (upper); 34; 47; 67 (both); 68; 69; 114 (upper). Courtesy of: Seabrook Wallcoverings, Inc. 1325 Farmville Road, Memphis, TN 38122, Retailers: 901-320-3500, Consumers: 800-238-9152, www.seabrookwallcoverings.com

Today Interiors: pages 8 (center); 13 (lower right); 17 (upper right); 19 (lower); 26 (upper left and lower left); 46 (full page). Courtesy of: Gaetano, exclusive importers of Today Interiors Wallcoverings, 186 Sherman Ave., Berkley Heights, NJ 07922, Phone: 908-508-9006, Fax: 908-508-9797, www.gaetano-usa.com

Village, a brand of F. Schumacher & Co.: pages 18 (left); 21; 23 (upper right). Courtesy of: Village Wallcoverings, 79 Madison Avenue, New York, NY 10016, Phone: 212-213-7900, Fax: 212-213-7640, Consumers: 800-988-7775, Retailers: 800-523-1200, www.villagehome.com

Waverly Wallcoverings, a division of F. Schumacher & Co.: pages 23 (lower left and lower right); 25 (lower); 27; 30 (upper); 114 (upper); 115. Courtesy of: Waverly Wallcoverings, 79 Madison Avenue, New York, NY 10016, Phone: 212-213-7900, Fax: 212-213-7640, Consumers: 800-988-7775, Retailers: 800-523-1200, www.decoratewaverly.com

A Note About Suppliers

Usually, the supplies you need for making the projects in Lark books can be found at your local craft supply store, discount mart, home improvement center, or retail shop relevant to the topic of the book. Occasionally, however, you may need to buy materials or tools from specialty suppliers. In order to provide you with the most up-to-date information, we have created a list of suppliers on our Web site, which we update on a regular basis. Visit us at www.larkbooks.com, click on "Craft Supply Sources," and then click on the relevant topic. You will find numerous companies listed with their web address and/or mailing address and phone number.

coauthors

Lyna Farkas is an assessor for the City and Guilds of London Decorative Painting and Restoration Program, as well as a teacher and consultant in the decorative arts. She designs and paints professionally for showrooms, commercial sites, and residences through her business, In the Spirit of Decorum, based in Asheville, North Carolina.

Paige Gilchrist is a full-time author and editor at Lark Books, where she specializes in home decorating. Some of her recent books include *Decorating Your First Apartment*, *Rooms Your Kids Will Love*, *The New Book of Table Settings*, and *Stylish Storage*.

contributors

Sara-Beth Black was previously an interior designer in Florida. She moved to the beautiful mountains of Asheville, North Carolina, with her husband and two lovely children and now spends her time doing various creative projects.

Megan Kirby was born in one of the nerve centers of sausage country, Youngstown, Ohio, in 1962. Although she now lives in North Carolina, another sausage state, she goes back to Youngstown frequently to check on the local product. She has recently purchased a house, and renovating it has led to some interesting experimentation with wallpaper.

Diana Light lives and works in the beautiful Blue Ridge Mountains of North Carolina. Her home studio, like her life, is surrounded by glittering glass in hundreds of forms, styles, and types. After earning her BFA in painting and printmaking, she extended her expertise to etching and painting fine-glass objects. She has contributed to numerous Lark books and is the coauthor of Lark's *The Weekend Crafter: Etching Glass*.

Jamesa B. Selleck runs a consulting service specializing in accessory design and manufacturing. She often uses ordinary objects for unintended purposes—a vintage piano stool might appear as a side table, or a sconce back plate can become a bathroom tissue holder. She enjoys creating intimate, sophisticated surroundings that welcome friends and family and comfort the soul.

Heather Smith is a teacher, freelance writer, and project designer in Asheville, North Carolina. She enjoys assignments that allow her to enhance and beautify overlooked and ordinary objects, people, and places—especially, when the process requires her to make a mess and get dirty.

Terry Taylor lives and works in Asheville, North Carolina, as an editor and a project coordinator for Lark Books. He is a prolific designer and exhibiting artist, and works in media ranging from metals and jewelry to paper crafts and mosaics. Some of the most recent Lark books to which he has contributed include *Creative Outdoor Lighting*, *Summer Style*, and *The Book of Wizard Craft*.

Derick Tickle teaches decorative painting and restoration in Asheville, North Carolina. Trained in England as an apprentice, he is an examiner and advisor for the City and Guilds of London in decorative painting. He has run workshops and seminars for TV set designers, interior decorators, and professionals in Britain, New Zealand, and the United States.

index